THE PULPIT AND THE PAPER

A PASTOR'S COMING OF AGE IN NEWSPRINT

ROBERT W. LEE

Smyth & Helwys Publishing, Inc.
6316 Peake Road
Macon, Georgia 31210-3960
1-800-747-3016
©2020 by Robert Wright Lee
All rights reserved.

Author Photo: Katelyn A. Byng

Library of Congress Cataloging-in-Publication Data

Names: Lee, Robert W. (Robert Wright), author.
Title: The pulpit and the paper : a pastor's coming of age in newsprint / by Robert W. Lee.
Other titles: Newspaper columns. Selections | Statesville record & landmark.
Description: Macon, GA : Smyth & Helwys Publishing, 2020. | Includes bibliographical references.
Identifiers: LCCN 2020042276 | ISBN 9781641732796 (paperback) | ISBN 9781641732802 (ebook)
Subjects: LCSH: Meditations.
Classification: LCC BV4832.3 .L44 2020 | DDC 242--dc23
LC record available at https://lccn.loc.gov/2020042276

Disclaimer of Liability: With respect to statements of opinion or fact available in this work of nonfiction, Smyth & Helwys Publishing Inc. nor any of its employees, makes any warranty, express or implied, or assumes any legal liability or responsibility for the accuracy or completeness of any information disclosed, or represents that its use would not infringe privately-owned rights.

Advance Praise for *The Pulpit and the Paper*

I try to listen to every sermon Rev. Rob Lee preaches, and I try to read everything he writes. Now that just got easier. This book is like a "Best Hits" album of one of America's great prophetic voices. As a descendent of General Robert E. Lee, Rob's life is helping heal the wounds of history. His message is a balm to the festering, untreated wound of American racism and hatred.

—Shane Claiborne
Author, activist, co-founder of Red Letter Christians

Journalism and preaching share a singular mission: to tell the truth. Rev. Rob Lee was born with a burdensome legacy, and much like many of our heroes, Rob chose to bear this burden in the most complex of ways. He chose not to bury the lede, but to run his ancestry as the front page headline above the fold. As a result, Rob has earned my trust. I believe him because his words are brave and courageous enough to bear the weight of truth. In this book, we have the benefit of hindsight. This anthology contains columns published years prior to Rob's invitation to address the nation in the wake of the Charlottesville riots. No prophet asks for the job, but it is clear that God was making a path for Rob's life and witness. This book holds tender, delightful, and profound stories that are as inspirational as they are true. The singular mission of the journalist and preacher is beautifully accomplished in this work.

—Rev. Mandy Sloan McDow
Senior Minister
Los Angeles First United Methodist Church

As I read *The Pulpit and the Paper*, I kept wondering, "How did Rob Lee write so much, and so well, and so insightfully, at such a young age?" I especially value this collection right now—when many of us are deeply disappointed in so many of the well-known religious leaders of the older generation. Thank God for Rob Lee, a preacher who doesn't just preach the good news, but also makes news with his penetrating and heartfelt message of justice, joy, and peace.

—Brian D. McLaren
Author of *Faith after Doubt*

Faith manifests in numerous ways, but, to the Rev. Rob Lee, his calling is to live his devotion publicly. My audience is always richer for hearing his unique perspective on the critical intersection of religion and social justice. This book is the evolution of a public figure who is willing to bare his wounds and to be honest about his struggle. Lee's journey from a hometown newspaper columnist to a pastor is deeply personal, yet familiar.

— Ali Velshi
Host of MSNBC's *Velshi*

Also by Robert W. Lee

Stained-Glass Millennials

A Sin by Any Other Name:
Reckoning with Racism and the Heritage of the South

*To Stephanie, my love, thank you for you.
Thank you for the newsprint we've cried over,
the newsprint we've laughed over,
and the newsprint we met over.
The best is yet to come.*

Acknowledgments

A book that compiles eight years of material and decides what is deemed worthy of reading out of those eight years is no easy task—and one I couldn't do by myself. I am eternally grateful to Samantha Cordialini and Mindy Grassal, who spent hours transcribing these articles from the original newsprint to a document that could be compiled. You both are amazing and wonderful. Mindy has also been an incredible PR representative during this time where life seems so crazy. Thank you both for being so patient and so persistent with your work with me.

There have been so many friends—both old and new—to whom I'm grateful as I compiled this book: Molly Smith for being a uniquely compassionate friend; Frankie Boyko for your encouragement, strength, and kindness; Ruwa Romman, how I could have done any of this without you is unfathomable; and Palmer Cantler for your consistent friendship and fiercely loyal hope in my work. Michele Gardner has always checked in on me while I'm writing. I'm also grateful to Sierra Ewing-Ashworth, who has shown me what forgiveness and new chances in friendship look like, and I'm grateful to Abbi Smithmyer, who continues to show me what a passion for learning and writing look like. A special shoutout to Katelyn Byng for the headshot on the back cover. I'm also grateful for clergy colleagues and mentors such as the Rev. Sarah Heath, the Rev. Mandy McDow, the Rev. Leo Morton, the Rev. Jeremy Cannada, and the Rev. Dr. Michael Gehring. While I know I missed people, I also want to thank my first PR representative and dear friend Ory Owen, who knew I wanted this project to happen but didn't get to see it through to completion on this side of heaven.

I am especially indebted to Chelsea Clinton for her introduction to this book. Chelsea has been and continues to be a source of strength, courage, and conviction for myself and this nation. I am in her debt for that and so much more.

To Dave Ibach, former editor of the *Statesville Record & Landmark*, your willingness to give me a chance in 2011, when I was a senior in high school, is one of the most amazing feats accomplished by a newspaper editor anywhere. Truly you deserve a Pulitzer for your patience and teaching kindness.

To Keith Gammons, Leslie Andres, and the entire team at Smyth & Helwys, you all believed in me and gave me my first published book almost four years ago. I am grateful you took that chance.

To places like Appalachian State University; Statesville, North Carolina; Broad Street United Methodist Church; Wine Maestro; and Red Buffalo, thank you for hosting and cultivating me into the person and pastor I am today. Scott and I grew up in the best town ever. Speaking of that, Scott—you are the best sibling I could ask for.

Is it weird to acknowledge a poodle friend in your work? I don't care if it is. Frank Lee, you sit with me while I'm writing, and I'm all the better for it.

To Nana and Mom—you always keep boxes of my articles; now you can just keep this book of the best ones. You're welcome.

To Granddaddy and Dad—thanks for being so committed to what you love. It shines through here.

CONTENTS

Introduction by Chelsea Clinton   1
Preface   5

ON ENDINGS AND BEGINNINGS   9
   Purple Ink and Restoring the Years   11
   Building a Bigger Table   13
   God and the Wedding at Cana   15
   All of Our Years Are Golden Years   17
   We Are Not Alone   19
   Author Talks "Inexplicable Peace" Despite Cancer Diagnosis   21
   God Is a Shining Light   25
   Yearning Call to Be a Saint at Home   27
   Being at Home Is a Mindset of Faith   29
   How Will They Remember You When You're Gone?   31
   Saints, a Reminder of Life's Beauty   33
   With Spring Comes New Life   35
   Looking Forward to a Future with Hope   37
   Funerals Restore Our Faith   39
   Is the Church Dying?   41
   What Food Means for Resurrection   43
   Leave Space for Transition   45
   To Dear Ole Duke, With Love   47
   Doug Eason's Faith Legacy   49
   Live Life in God's Time   51
   An Interview with Dr. Stanley Hauerwas   53
   Love Is the Way Home   55
   Do All Dogs Go to Heaven?   57
   Conversations Can Change Perspectives   59
   On the Eve of Something Glorious: To Stephanie's Grandmother   61

MOMENTS THAT DEFINED A JOURNEY — 63
Friendship and Faith Are Important to God — 65
Thoughts on World Suicide Prevention Day — 67
Shabbat Shalom, Y'all — 71
Remember Your Baptism and Be Thankful — 73
Working Together Is a Sign of God's Kingdom — 75
Though Much Is Taken, Much Abides — 77
Embody Faith this Season — 79
The Precarious Position of Church — 81
Equality Is Part of God's Dream for the World — 83
Public Theology and Taylor Swift — 85
To Stephanie, on the Occasion of Our Wedding — 87
Faith and the Confederate Flag — 89

HOLIDAYS AND HOLY DAYS — 91
The Lights of Hanukkah Burn Bright, Renew Faith — 93
Sharing Faith: Be More Like Howard Adler — 95
O Little Town of Statesville — 97
What Matters Most in Life Isn't Tangible — 99
The Christmas Spirit, Alive in Each of Us — 101
The Hustle and Bustle of Christmas — 103
We Need the Hope of Christmas Now — 105
If Not Now, When? — 107
Wedding Planning Teaches about Lent — 109
An Invitation to Slow Down during Lent — 111
Lent Is a Time to Adjust — 113
Mark Lent Faithfully — 115
God Is Present in the Silence — 117
Lent and Finding Faith in *Family Guy* — 119
Make the Most of Holy Week — 121
Passover Is a Time to Talk about Freedom — 123
The Goodness Found Friday — 125
A Column Turned Prayer for Ascension Sunday — 127
Pentecost and the Klan — 129
Where Will You Place Your Faith on Election Day? — 131
The Church, the Kingdom, and Ordinary Time — 133
Christ the King Sunday: The End of the Church Year — 135
On the Anniversary of a Tragedy (September 11, 2001) — 137

ISSUES OF CONSEQUENCE AND FAITH   139

"Building a Bridge": An interview with Father James Martin   141
Peace with Justice   145
Facing Mental Illness with Faith   149
Orlando, Liturgy, and Action   151
Be Strong and Courageous   153
Education Is a Faith Issue   155
Interview: Theologian and Thinker Diana Butler Bass   157
To Get to Heaven, You Have to Know Your Geography   161
Disease of Addiction Must Be Addressed by Faith Community   163
God Is Not Done with Us Yet   165
God Is Glorified through Music   167
Make Welcome the Refugee in Your Midst   169
Practice Your Business Faithfully   171
Give Faithfully to the Work of God   173
God and Politics   175
Jesus and the Immigrant Children   177
Different Ideologies in Faith   179
God's Peace Is Important to Faith   181
Thanking God for Second Chances   183

GROUNDED IN FAITH AND SCRIPTURE   185

Stay Grounded in Faith   187
Worshiping During the Week   189
Learning to Walk on Water   191
Use Your Time Wisely   193
Don't Let People Rob You of Your Joy   195
Find Sacred Spaces and Relationships   197
Reading Scripture Is Important to Our Faith   199
Disappointments Fuel Our Faith   201
The Effort to Live a Life Worthy of Faith   203
The Art of Listening   205
Listening Is an Act of Faith   207
God Created the Sabbath for a Reason: Finding Peace   209
Small-town Construction   211
God's Answer to Anxiety Is Faith   213
God Cares about Your Soul   215
In Remembrance, There Is Life   217
Your Faith Letter of Reference   219

Challenges Are Part of Life	221
Faith Is a Lesson in Slowing Down, Learning to Read Again	223

SERMONS OF PUBLIC THEOLOGY — 225
Harvard University's Memorial Church	227
Ebenezer Baptist Church: The Pulpit of Dr. King	233
Maranatha Baptist Church: With Former President Jimmy Carter	239

SUMMING UP MY ONE SERMON — 245
Faith in Appalachia: A Lesson in Storytelling	247
The Advent of the Stars	251
Let's Focus on the Real Conversation	253
Our Lives Are Defined by Love	255

> "Four hostile newspapers are more to be
> feared than a thousand bayonets."
> —Napoleon Bonaparte

From the letters to the editor in the *Statesville Record & Landmark*:

September 21, 2017

I wanted to take the time to shed some light on recent events and this false prophet Rev. Rob Lee.

What an atrocity to our state. He has resigned from his position in the church after his speech on the VMAs was not as well received as he thought it would be. Then after all that [he] went on "The View" to talk about himself. Maybe that works in places like California and New York but now it has become about making a name for himself. He used resigning from his church as a way for people to feel sorry for him.

This is the South, it is history. Any Civil War-era church with a cemetery, will have Confederate flags. If we don't teach our children about Gen. Lee and the Civil War history is bound to repeat itself. We live in a world where its [*sic*; it's] just easier to take down statues and then forget about the history and why they were placed there to begin with. This is contributing to the dumbing down of America. This is all over statutes [*sic*; statues] of men who have long been dead.

The South has a deep history with the Civil War. If you don't like it, don't look at it. Don't live in a place that is that rich with history and try to change that. It happened, nothing can change it. —Samantha Honeycutt, Statesville[†]

[†] Samantha Honeycutt to editor, Statesville.com, September 17, 2017 (statesville.com/news/letter-rev-rob-lee-doesn-t-respect-our-history/article_8cc93e14-9f0b-11e7-aa19-a39939f1e3b4.html). Original punctuation and spelling retained with bracketed editorial clarifications.

INTRODUCTION
BY CHELSEA CLINTON

It is rare to read a walk through someone's life as their heart and conscience develops. Yet that is exactly what this book is. It's not a memoir or autobiography; there is no overarching narrative. Instead, it is a series of meditations on what was on Rob's mind and in his heart at various moments, some reacting to events of his day or "the day" and others the result of long-ruminated-on questions. Rob became a columnist for his local paper in 2011, when he was a senior in high school, and vaulted onto the national stage at the 2017 MTV Video Music Awards, speaking with the mother of Heather Heyer, a woman murdered at a counter-protest to the Confederate-loving neo-Nazi-embracing hate rally in Charlottesville earlier that month.

Throughout the book, it is clear that Rob never thought he would be famous, even after his riveting moment on the MTV stage, after the horrible hate he received from those who privileged their whiteness over our humanity, and after his clear courage in how he stood up to that hate and stood for the future he wants to live in—even as it cost him his job at the pulpit. The absence of expectation of fame doesn't mean Rob has no expectations. It is clear that he expects himself to do better and be better each day—and sometimes that he will do that tomorrow in a literal sense, and other times it may be over many tomorrows, but it will always happen, as Rob will not cease until it does. This is a serious book but not one that is burdened by being serious. It is full of joy and possibility and calls us all to believe in our tomorrows.

In his columns, Rob discusses events in his own life, from a brother's opera performance to his wedding, and seminal events in other people's lives that he presided over as a pastor, from baptisms to weddings to funerals. One of the most beautiful entries is one where Rob as a human being converges with Rob as a pastor, at least as it reads to me; it is the letter he wrote his wife's grandmother as she waited for her own transition to the hereafter. Another is Rob's recitation of what his wife had already taught him before they exchanged vows. He frames the lessons he learned with and from Stephanie in biblical references, and yet he does not make them exclusive to the two of them or their shared faith. His experience is as a Christian, and while he shares stories and lessons he likely learned across his home, school, worship, and academic work here and elsewhere in the book, he invites any reader into his experience with an open heart.

It is clear throughout his writing and preaching that Rob's world is shaped by his relationship to God, Scripture, his faith community, his church. He does not believe my world or yours has to be shaped by the same, and he believes there is a danger, which far too many Christians today have fallen into in Rob's estimation, of worshiping the Bible rather than God. That understanding is likely why Rob has angered so many people when he draws inspiration beyond the Bible, including from Taylor Swift. Perhaps paradoxically, Rob finds similar solace in practicing stillness, in nature as well as in Swift's lyrics and her call to "shake it off." All of these help orient Rob where he wants to be and hopes any of us could be, focused on the future and, for Rob, on his calling in life to help build a bigger table in every sense. The varied ways in which Rob reenergizes and balances stress with joy hopefully help any reader feel more comfortable and confident in how we do the same.

Family, friends, and those he admires, from poet Maya Angelou to Bertha Hamilton, the nurse assistant at a local hospital, also helped build Rob's world and influenced how he experiences it. We meet many of those he admires in his columns, and each rumination on what they have meant to him, each shared conversation, is a glimpse into Rob's journey to fulfill his calling. A polaroid of discovery.

Throughout the book, Rob's gift of taking what may feel abstract or irrelevant and grounding such questions and lessons in more accessible language and analogy is evident. A favorite example of that is when he talks about the meaning of Lent and a trip to the chiropractor in the same column. It may not have been an obvious pairing, but it makes sense in Rob's telling. The "making sense of" is another of Rob's gifts on display throughout the book, as is making clear how his meditations relate to culture today and the culture that shaped him, from discussing his favorite movies (spoiler alert: one is *A River Runs Through It*) to why a scene in *Family Guy* meant so much to him to the insight he finds in *Star Trek: Generations*.

Rob apologizes for his family's sins of enslaving people and devaluing human life. There is no caveat; there is no "but." There is only an "and," the accompanying calling for a greater understanding of our shared responsibility to ensure and protect human life and dignity, whether your last name is Lee or Clinton or anything else. For Rob, this is fundamental to his understanding of his faith. While he feels a particular responsibility to dismantle white supremacy in our country because of his family's history, he also clearly feels it is the responsibility of all white people and, given his calling, all Christians. Rob clearly believes the church should be synonymous with solidarity, and he is motivated in part because he knows that is not the way many Christians, especially many white Christians, feel today. One column focuses on how he does not believe it is Christian to refuse to shop at stores owned by LGBTQ+ Americans and that such an affront to human dignity is itself un-Christian.

This book resonates with me for many reasons, including its honesty, bravery, humor, and humility. It also resonates because I share Rob's conviction that we need a progressive public theology or, at the least, progressive Christians whose faith informs our views on climate change, women's rights, voting rights, immigrant and asylum seekers' rights, education, health care, and the government's responsibility to do more to protect and provide equal rights, protection, and opportunities than it currently does or ever has. Rob's words and his example urge progressive Christians to work for what we believe is right and be unapologetic about sharing our reasons for doing so, including our faith. As Rob notes in one column, education is a faith issue, and he doesn't mean—while he doesn't say this—fighting about the Pledge of Allegiance. He means teaching kids to think for themselves, be courageous, and nourish their bodies and their civic spirits.

While Rob doesn't put faith in politicians to always do that or to do so alone, without public pressure, he certainly knows when it is important to stand against politicians—and anyone—who stoke hatred or whose policies hurt people. This is an evolution Rob's columns show clearly. Earlier in his writing career, he doesn't criticize politicians he disagrees with or praise those he sees as doing good work by name. In later columns, he calls out President Donald Trump for peddling "cheap grace." He speaks openly of his admiration of Congresswoman Alexandria Ocasio-Cortez and his honor in meeting her. Rob doesn't shy away from the death threat he received after writing about his meeting with Congresswoman Ocasio-Cortez, nor does he glorify it as some badge of honor. He merely thanks the local government for their response and calls for more "big-hearted" people. He had a similar public reaction to his firing after the MTV speech and the death threats he received then, meeting that moment with courage: "I lost my job and found my soul."

About halfway through the book, Rob quotes Diana Butler Bass, a theologian he admires and later interviews, as once reminding him that "God is the unfinished sentence." He later asks Dr. Butler Bass what she meant by that. What is clear from reading this collection of Rob's writing is that his life is very much an unfinished sentence yet one already full of verbs, with a bias toward action to dismantle white supremacy, tear down misogyny, protect the vulnerable, and grow the table so all can join with equal dignity. That does not detract from God being omnipresent and simultaneously beyond, always calling us forward. *The Pulpit and the Paper* is not a peaceful book, as Rob knows that our tomorrows are in jeopardy unless we act differently and urgently, as he consistently urges us to do. Yet, for all its vital exhortations, this is a book full of joy, of love, of possibility. It is also a fantastic antidote to all those framed portraits of a Nordic-looking, sparkly white-skinned, commercial-worthy, brown-hair-flowing Jesus that were on the walls of my Sunday school classroom. That man as depicted never existed. Rob writes that he "wanted to be a different preacher, a better preacher." He already is, and he will be. Read this book, share this book, return to this book, love deeply, build a bigger table, and create better tomorrows.

PREFACE

Don't you wish you had a job like mine? All you have to do is think up a certain number of words!
—American columnist Dave Barry

I never intended to be a newspaper columnist—or a public theologian for that matter. I never intended anything I've done that ended up being consequential. Except one thing . . . I love telling stories, and storytelling matters to me. I think I always intended to be a preacher—that always pairs well with storytelling. All we have are our stories. They make us who we are, and though we won't make it out of this human existence alive, we'll make it out with our stories—at least we hope so. There is something uniquely human about the preservation of our particular narratives because those stories define who we are. With that reality, I'm mindful that stories can end quite abruptly, and, in the midst of pain and despair, stories can loom like specters, haunting us through the hallways of what we've always known.

I grew up in a town of 28,000 people in North Carolina. With the exception of my time in undergrad and seminary (totaling seven of my twenty-eight years), I have lived here. Unlike those who left this town after high school, I returned. I get the question, "Why did you move back to a backwards place?" Well, that place, regardless of what they think, is my home. I confess that coming of age here hasn't been easy. There is real pain and sorrow, but they are coupled with the hope that we must be better for the future's sake.

It was the hope I found in Statesville that took me to Inglewood, California in August 2017. After someone at MTV heard me on NPR, they invited me to speak at the Video Music Awards. I stood on the stage, the red light clicked, and I spoke in front of over 5.6 million viewers—the biggest pulpit in the course of my short life. That moment has defined the years since, changing the lens through which I see the world. I started thinking about what led me to such a public moment, how the preacher from small-town North Carolina became the pastor to MTV. For me, the very public speech I gave there (and later on ABC's talk show *The View*) was in large part due to something that doesn't require speech at all; in fact, all it required was a word processor and a willing newspaper editor.

In 2011, during my free block at Statesville High School, I realized there was no way I would meet the required service hours by just sitting there. I decided to write the editor of the *Statesville Record & Landmark* about a previous response someone had given to the paper. Frustrated that our community was only hearing the Evangelical voice and the Fundamentalist narrative, I admonished the editor to consider that there were other realities within the Christian lexicon, that all of our narratives didn't converge at the Evangelical epicenter. Later that day I received the opposite of what I thought I'd get: Dave Ibach, then-editor of the *Statesville Record & Landmark*, offered me a job as the paper's religion columnist. As with any news organization, the funds were skimpy, so I wouldn't be paid. It didn't matter to me; I had a bona fide job as a religion columnist at age eighteen. I was certain the Pulitzer was in my future.

I couldn't have realized it then, but now I recognize that taking a chance and gaining a voice started me on a trajectory of events that lead to the MTV stage. And even after MTV, that same newspaper published an op-ed (see p. 253) I wrote to shift the narrative of the conversation. That op-ed ran the same day I appeared on national television with Whoopi Goldberg and Joy Behar on ABC's *The View*. It's amazing how stories that end often end at the beginning of a new chapter.

That's what is so special to me about this book: you will see my own fears met with the world's expectations. You will see how my views develop. I can't get everything perfectly right, but I take seriously the notion that I must continue to be present in a community I love. Every time a job or opportunity comes by that would take me away from Statesville, I think back to these columns and the conversations (both good and bad) that they fostered in the community. People frequently comment on an article that resonates with them and how it makes them feel.

Still, I am not without controversy in my hometown. The first followers of Jesus weren't without controversy either. I may not have it all figured out, but I'm working on it, and I invite you to join me in this anthology and maybe find yourself there. This is a testament to the fact that following Jesus requires you to be a rough draft, never complete, and always in need of an editor.

So, dear reader, I'm left with gratitude knowing that this volume is incomplete. There's all the more to write, to learn, to understand, and to tell. These pages contain a small portion of my writing career, but it is so formative that I believed it deserved its own book. When a writer first gains his voice, you recognize what really matters to them. It's said that Eugene Peterson once quipped that preachers only have one sermon—one story they tell repeatedly over the course of their pastorates. I used to scoff at that. I wanted to be a different preacher, a better preacher. But then I learned that the stories we tell over and over are the stories we care about most deeply.

Statesville is a small town where "fancy" isn't in the town vocabulary. My grandmother kept the clippings that my team helped transcribe to make this book possible. These newspaper clippings and sermon snippets won't solve the world's problems or create abiding and lasting peace among the nations, but it will tell a story, and stories are where things begin . . . and end. This is my most personal work thus far because you see the growth and struggle, the joy and pain. Ultimately, it is where I have found God and God has found me. I wish you peace, hope, and courage as we all continue to craft our stories.

—The Rev. Robert "Rob" W. Lee
October 2020

ON ENDINGS AND BEGINNINGS

"Since when," he asked,
"Are the first line and last line of any poem
Where the poem begins and ends?"

—*Seamus Heaney*
(*from "The Fragment," in* Electric Light)

Our existence is defined by the realities that give us life and by those that could take life from us. These articles seek to show the hopes and fears we see in those endings and beginnings. Whether it was the loss of someone close or the beginning of a new life chapter, we see the beauty of what God can do whether the situation seems horrific or too good to be true.

PURPLE INK AND RESTORING THE YEARS

OCTOBER 25TH, 2017

What do you do when eight years have passed since an event that changed your life forever? I don't know if I was ever fully able to grieve the loss of my friend Abbey because I was busy being a pastoral presence for others. I'm taking consolation this year in an obscure verse from Joel that I first heard the great preacher Sam Wells preach from years ago. The prophet Joel in the second chapter of the book says,

> I will repay you for the years
>   that the swarming locust has eaten,
> the hopper, the destroyer, and the cutter,
>   my great army, which I sent against you.
> You shall eat in plenty and be satisfied,
>   and praise the name of the Lord your God,
>   who has dealt wondrously with you.
> And my people shall never again be put to shame.
> You shall know that I am in the midst of Israel,
>   and that I, the Lord, am your God and there is no other.
> And my people shall never again be put to shame. (vv. 25-27, NRSV)

This past month, on a beautiful September eve in Statesville, I officiated the wedding of my late friend's sister, Anna, and the love of her life, Zach. God was in the process of restoring the years. We ate, we danced, we celebrated, and we remembered. Though we could never fully resurrect in this life that person we loved so dearly, we could restore and redeem the situation through our livelihoods and the gift we've been given to stay on this earth and live out Abbey's legacy.

Life is a struggle; that much is certain. But the saints remind us that "we feebly struggle, they in glory shine" (to borrow from the great hymn), and that is the greatest hope we have.[1] I've learned so much since Abbey left this world for the hereafter, and there is so much I wish I could tell her. But the hope of the resurrection is that one day I will be able to tell her these things. She'll hear of Stephanie, my wife, and she'll hear of the debacle and drama I've found myself in. She will laugh at the things we used to laugh at.

I pulled down my yearbook from the year before Abbey died the other day, and scribbled in iconic purple ink were these words: "Roberto, let me just tell you I have no idea what I would have done without you this year! I mean who would I have to pick on, and who would pick on me? I'm so glad we've gotten to know each other, these next few years will be great, but it's only the beginning of something crazy, I love you, Abbey."

I don't know if a young sixteen-year-old named Abbey knew that our friendship and her death would change my ministry in my hometown forever. I don't think it was that obvious to anyone. But God has restored the years that the locust has taken away. And I stand as a testament to the awesome grace of God because of saints now gone from our sight like Abbey.

So this week, the week of the anniversary of her death, I am remembering her . . . I am not letting go. I know it may seem odd to cultivate a moment that happened eight years ago on a fateful Halloween, but I know that in the end, all we have are the stories and events that transpired in our lives. We offer them to God in the hopes that they will be transformed into something restorative.

I will never understand these things. I will never understand why a bad thing could happen to such a beautiful person, but in the end, I will remember this week and the anniversary of her death for as long as I have breath in my lungs and a pulse in my body. That is one of my gifts to this world, and I refuse to let it be forgotten.

Rest well, Abbey, and rise in glory.

---

1. William Walsham How, "For All the Saints" (1864).

BUILDING A BIGGER TABLE

OCTOBER 26, 2017

On November 1, we mark what is to me one of the holiest days of the year: All Saints' Day. There is a certain beauty in remembering the past and those who have journeyed forward beyond our sight, and there is a certain beauty in remembering that we, too, will one day have the shadows lengthen on our own lives. We live caught between the certainty of death and the promise of life.

The realities force us to ask what we value in life. This past week, Stephanie and I went to San Diego and worshiped at Pilgrim United Church of Christ. One of the hymns we sang gave me chills:

> For everyone born, a place at the table,
> to live without fear, and simply to be,
> to work, to speak out, to witness and worship,
> for everyone born, the right to be free,
> and God will delight when we are creators
> of justice and joy, compassion and peace:
> yes, God will delight when we are creators
> of justice, justice and joy![2]

We live in a world with short tables and hard realities for so many people right here in Statesville. We live in a world where the condition of your birth determines your place (or lack thereof) at the table. Perhaps we can start to build a bigger table.

---

2. Shirley Erena Murray, "For Everyone Born, a Place at the Table" (Carol Stream, IL: Hope Publishing Company, 1998).

I have a friend named Brian who created a beautiful table for Stephanie and me after we were married. It has plenty of space for friends and family to join us. We wouldn't be content with a table small enough for just the two of us; we need space to share—and our world does, too. Because, as the great Bill Coffin once said, "The world is too dangerous for anything but truth and too small for anything but love."

So, this week, as we mark the leaves dying to the ground, may we marvel at the beauty of the mysteries of life. We all deserve to have a spot at the table of grace. The table has been made ready, and we must set a place for everyone in love and acceptance.

GOD AND THE WEDDING AT CANA

OCTOBER 2017

I love a good wedding. In fact, this Saturday I will be attending one of my good friend's nuptials. We all have been to a wedding; we've all enjoyed seeing happiness. This reminded me of a story we often hear of Jesus beginning his earthly ministry with none other than a wedding.

I must admit that when it comes to big crowds, I can be somewhat of an introvert. Now don't get me wrong: I can put on my extrovert hat and "work the crowd" just as well as anyone else, but I feel sometimes like Jesus did, hesitant to make a scene when it's easier to sit by the punch bowl and talk with close friends. As Jesus said, "My hour has not yet come." But there is something interesting about John 2:4 , something profound that we often miss when gleaning through the New Testament.

Interestingly enough, it is suggested that most of the water in the time of Jesus' life and teachings was not fit to drink. People in his time didn't know what we know about purification. Christ, the one we call Lord, took unclean, undrinkable water and made it into wine, which the Jews considered to be fit for drinking. How marvelous! Jesus took something dirty and made something beautiful! How often do we sit on the sidelines and expect transformation? How often do we just wait for God to send a sign? God is in our midst, working now! God is in the business of taking something ordinary, like dirty water, and making it extraordinary, like the good wine.

Dr. Samuel Wells, the Dean of Duke Chapel, puts it this way: "The best advice I can offer is that it's not love that teaches you what marriage means—it's marriage that teaches you what love means." We are constantly learning, constantly transforming, and that is the beauty of the wedding at Cana. Jesus came out of his shell in the sense that he found the transforming power of ministry. We too must be willing not to wait for our hour to come but to bring that hour about!

The next time you're at a wedding, look at the transformative power of what is happening. Two beings are becoming one. It is truly marvelous and appropriate that Jesus would start his ministry at a wedding. God invites us, if we are willing, to become one with our Maker. God invites us to transform our lives and the lives of others into "good wine."

I really am looking forward to my friends' wedding, and I wish them all the best for a happy future. There is something to be said about being willing to commit your life to someone else. I certainly don't claim to be the foremost scholar or experienced practitioner of marriage, but what I do know is this: God, like a groom, is waiting at the end of the aisle. Are you willing to walk towards the beauty and splendor of a future in God's kingdom? That, my friends, is a wedding we can all look forward to.

ALL OF OUR YEARS ARE GOLDEN YEARS

JUNE 2011

A few years back, my friend and I were interviewed side by side for a documentary done by the North Carolina Baptist Aging Ministries. We were young, happy, and talking about working with senior adults in our community. Years later, I still think about that video. My friend isn't here anymore on this side of heaven. She didn't have the opportunity to grow older and into her golden years like so many people will have the opportunity to do.

I think her death started to put things into perspective for me. We've all taken days, months, and even years for granted. We grow older with each passing day, but do we really realize the wonder and amazement of having another morning of life? I've developed three points to help me grow older. I hope that these might help you as we continue to journey on the road of life.

1. *Recognize that joy is holy.* We sing about joy in church, with such standards as "Joy to the World" and "Joyful, Joyful, We Adore Thee." But do we know what joy is? Joy is that feeling on Easter or Christmas morning when we realize that this is life at its best. Joy is that ability to stand at the ocean or in the mountains and see the majesty of the creation of God. Joy is that inescapable feeling that things are right in our world.

2. *Be vulnerable.* We as a culture have gotten in a mentality that we have to do everything for ourselves. Any lack of independence is a sign of defeat. But ultimately, we need to be vulnerable. Some of the most important experiences we have as human beings are finding the wounds of another person and touching the heart of that wound. We stand in moments of time and find ourselves growing older, and in our vulnerability we can express our fears and our joys about the aging process. People need to shift

their realities from independence to interdependence. God weaves God's presence through each and every one of us. God is present in our aging joys and aging sorrows. Ultimately, if we are vulnerable enough, we find God in ourselves and in the people around us.

3. *Love like there's no tomorrow.* None of us are guaranteed tomorrow. Nothing is certain in this life, and nothing will be able to prevent the inevitable from happening. That may sound bleak, but it gives us the opportunity to love like there's no tomorrow. We can love friends, spouses, children, grandchildren, churches, and communities in ways that point to the beautiful love God has for each of us. It will never be as perfect as God's love, but that doesn't mean we shouldn't try. Love is what gets us through those long days and cold nights. Love is what allows us to age with grace and dignity, so to love like there's no tomorrow enables us to age as people of grace, hope, and faith.

Growing older shouldn't scare us; growing bitter or hateful should scare us. For in our older years we see the fruition of God's work in our lives. God showed the fruition of God's promise to Abraham in the last years of his life. In the end, God sees all our years as golden years—years that allow us to be God's presence here on earth.

Even though my friend isn't here anymore, I am reminded of that documentary. I know I am twenty years old; I am by no means in my older years. But I hope in God's grace that I will be able to experience all the joys that are ahead. The beauty of marriage, the pitter-patter of children and grandchildren. And I've always wanted to go to the English countryside. I take with me the memory of my friend as a reminder that getting old is a luxury some people will never have.

There's an old hymn that became iconic in the 1960s, and it goes like this: "God of our weary years, God of our silent tears, thou who hast brought us thus far on the way; thou who hast by thy might led us into the light, keep us forever in the path, we pray."[3] Let us give thanks for everything we have, our weary years and our silent tears, but also let us give thanks that we are given the opportunity to laugh and find joy, to be vulnerable, and to love like there's no tomorrow.

---

3. James Weldon Johnson, "Lift Every Voice and Sing," 1900, www.pbs.org/black-culture/explore/black-authors-spoken-word-poetry/lift-every-voice-and-sing/.

WE ARE NOT ALONE

JULY 2011

A 1994 movie was filmed in Wilmington, North Carolina, that is remembered more for the accidental shooting death of Brandon Lee, Bruce Lee's son, than anything else. During the movie, *The Crow*, one of the characters makes a remark: "If the people we love are stolen from us, the way to have them live on is to never stop loving them. Buildings burn, people die, but real love is forever."

I went to a funeral this past week for a man by the name of Jack Sherrill. Jack was an active member of my church and was influential in my faith. His passing struck me as I was pondering this road of life. I am of the mindset that there is no greater honor than to be with someone in their final moments or to remember them after they are gone. Frederick Buechner, the Presbyterian minister, once preached in a sermon, "Christ came to us in the countless disguises through people who one way or another strengthened us, judged us, comforted us, healed us, by the power of Christ alive within them." I often look back on my years and see the impact of people who are now part of the kingdom of God fully and completely.

Death is scary. It is the reality we must face because it is a reality that comes to all of us. But there is a wonderful creed that says, "In life, in death, in life beyond death, we are not alone. God is with us." In that reality we see on the horizon, we must live life with real love—love that is beyond measure. Maybe that love is for the partner we have in life, the church we call home, or the simple things that make us happy. I once was able to ask my favorite theologian some questions. One of my questions was about death. Dr. Stanley Hauerwas, professor of ethics at Duke Divinity School, has studied dying, and I asked him how we can live prepared to die. He replied, "I'm not sure if Christians today can live lives such that they are ready to die. We simply no longer know how to do that. We can, however, keep before us people that are long gone. That can never be forgotten. Just to the extent that we remember this, we continue to have hope that we too will be faithful as we face death."

I can remember that when I was little, my former pastor would notify us of a death in our congregation by saying the person transferred their membership from our church to the church triumphant. We too will transfer our membership, and that is something we shouldn't fear but embrace. Live life like we're ready to die. Live because we are full of love.

I would be remiss in my duties as a columnist not to mention the release of *Harry Potter and the Deathly Hallows: Part 2*. The movie series that helped define a generation ended this past week with the release of this final film. There is a great scene in which Professor Dumbledore tells Harry Potter, "Do not pity the dead, Harry. Pity the living, and, above all, those who live without love." Dumbledore said it best. Love until you can't love anymore, and then your life will be worth living, and remember to live, as Shakespeare once penned long ago, "Seeing that death, a necessary end, will come when it will come."

AUTHOR TALKS "INEXPLICABLE PEACE" DESPITE CANCER DIAGNOSIS

MARCH 9, 2018

Dr. Kate Bowler is a friend and professor at Duke University Divinity School. Most recently, she is a *New York Times* best-selling author for her book, *Everything Happens for a Reason: And Other Lies I've Loved*.

Kate was diagnosed with stage 4 colon cancer and has had to face some hard and difficult truths. Through it all, she has shown the fortitude and hope it takes to face odds that are bleak. She has faced them with the most dignity and grace I have ever seen. Her book is full of timeless truths about facing illness, finding God, and seeing what really matters in life. I commend it to you all. I sat down with Kate and asked her some questions about her struggle and what we can learn from it.

Q: *You're a wonderful professor, a gifted writer, and a person of great fortitude who has faced insurmountable odds. What's one piece of advice for those struggling with illness or simply trying to get to tomorrow?*

Kate Bowler: Thank you, Rob. There isn't one solution for everyone in every situation, but I would say not to let anyone dictate a reason for your terrible thing. The moment something horrible happens, well-meaning people are tempted to rush in with a justification for why you're suffering—maybe you're being punished by God, or you didn't use enough SPF Chapstick or eat enough quinoa. I've come to understand that we are all looking for control over the exhaustion of helplessness. So don't let someone give you a reason for your suffering, especially if it absolves them of holding your hand through hard times.

Q: What have you learned about God's love in the face of your diagnosis and journey?
KB: I felt God so clearly in the care of other people. These years have taught me true gratitude and occasionally have given me an inexplicable peace I can only attribute to God. There were moments when chaos descended, and I should have felt nauseous with fear. Instead I felt overwhelming love. Like the moment I first got my diagnosis and was heading into surgery, I turned to my husband and knew in my marrow I loved him. I didn't expect to live twelve hours, let alone years of our promised life together. But instead of fear . . . love. That could only be God.

Q: If you could give encouragement to spouses and children of those who may be facing a situation similar to yours, what would you want them to know?
KB: Your presence is the best gift. Not many people want to walk up to the edge of the cliff with people in pain. The ones that hold your shoulder and match your steps all the way forward are the true saints. Thank you for being at our sides.

Q: Through it all, you remain an "incurable optimist," and many, including those who might be cynical, could see that as blind faith. What do you say to that?
KB: I don't really have the luxury of cynicism. I've got things to do and people to love.

Q: What has sustained you in this journey?
KB: My friends and family. I am lucky to be surrounded by far cleverer, compassionate, and intelligent people who still want to be seen with me in public. These fabulous people have carried me through the shadows and held my sorrow and joy in equal regard. They are the reason I still bother with lipstick, know all the words to "Eye of the Tiger," made it through dozens of scans and surgeries, and know how to sneak Starbucks into the ICU. They've all earned their starry crowns.

Q: What has drained you?
KB: Cancer treatment. It's super gross.

Q: *What's one word you'd use to describe the God you have come to know in this?*
KB: Persistent.

GOD IS A SHINING LIGHT

OCTOBER 2011

In the Jewish faith, when our Jewish brothers and sisters visit a grave, the custom is to place a small stone on the grave. This shows that someone visited the grave site and that the deceased has not been forgotten.

When I was a young child, my grandmother would take me to play in Oakwood Cemetery. We'd play on the tree we affectionately knew as Moses, because of its age and size. As I grew, I stopped playing in the cemetery. I looked back on those days and marveled at the fact that I played in the cemetery, a place where I would later come to bury my uncle and a place where I would come to assist in many graveside services.

Around these shorter days, my mind often turns to death. Two years ago around this time, I lost a friend. I remember where I was and what I was doing when I received the call that my friend Abbey had died. I remember the gathering, the crying, and the pain. We all just wanted to rewind, to relive, and to never have to face death. We all have had experiences like these when we would give anything for more time.

God, in infinite wisdom, sent us examples, game-changers, people who expose the love affair God has with humanity. I am reminded of the words of the prophet Isaiah: "The people who walked in darkness have seen a great light; those who lived in a land of deep darkness, on them light has shined" (Isa 9:2). For me and many of my friends, we look back on the life that was lived when we remember Abbey Tsumas as a person who shined light on things. We remember that she has not been forgotten.

There is a creative writing professor [and NC Poet Laureate, 2012–2014] at Appalachian State University by the name of Joseph Bathanti. He tells the story of his friend who was in the business of restoring icons and sacred art. In one poem, Bathanti describes the brokenness of a statue that his friend was rebuilding. I would propose to you right now that God is in the business of restoring sacred art. God is at work in the very lives of broken people like you and me. God knows the hurt we feel when we are at a loss. God is ever present, ever ready to provide comfort and peace to those in need. It may not always be evident, but it is there, in our very midst.

I challenge you this week to adopt a tradition of remembrance. Maybe that's looking through an old photo album or paying a visit to a family member who has lost someone close. Maybe that's placing a stone on the grave of a loved one. For one day, we will all be laughing at death in our resurrection; we will giggle at tombstones and share stories around the graves. We will run, we will laugh, and, yes, we will shout for joy when we see people like Abbey again. We once again will be playing in the cemeteries.

YEARNING CALL TO BE A SAINT AT HOME

AUGUST 1, 2011

One Sunday, I heard a wonderful duet of "Shall We Gather at the River?"[4] I don't know about you, but when I think of that song I yearn for newness, to be one of those saints: "Yes, we'll gather at the river, the beautiful, beautiful river; gather with the saints at the river that flows by the throne of God."

Have you ever yearned for resurrection? Have you ever yearned to be a saint? I know I have. I have yearned to feel that saintly resurrection. To be a part of that great cast of people long gone or still here, to be a part of those people who push for justice, peace, and love in our community. That is something I could get used to.

I know where we can start our journey to sainthood. I believe sainthood has its roots where it once did, in the church. Dr. James Howell, pastor of Myers Park United Methodist Church, an amazing pastor, colleague, and theologian, once wrote,

> A church family can be—or is!—just as dysfunctional, loony and codependent as any other family. And yet, a family loves, a family sticks with you; you're stuck with each other, and the friction polishes us so we can more brilliantly reflect the love of Christ to the world. A church family knows how to deliver a casserole, join a prayer chain, or show up when needed; a family is exhilarated over the arrival of a new family member, and we are unusually attentive to the elderly or anybody who is sick.

---

4. Robert Lowry (1864).

I often cringe when people talk about the institution of the church being for a bygone generation bent on the old way. The liveliness of faith is in the institution formed by the people. Christianity, contrary to popular belief, is not a solitary religion. As one artist put it, "we live in the vast canopy woven by the ages." We live in the great chain of faith, connecting one generation of faith to another.

In the hymn "For All the Saints," we lustily sing, "O blest communion, fellowship divine! We feebly struggle, they in glory shine; for all are one in Thee, for all are Thine. Alleluia!"[5] Something about feeble struggle excites me. I may be a church nerd, but that is something we can all get into. What if, for instance, we were more a part of the institution that society has grown a distaste for? What if, instead of complaining about the church, we feebly struggle for the saints of God, for the church we used to love? That is faith that recharges the heart and soul.

I have a newsflash. Yes, life-changing news. You don't have to be dead to be a saint! There are people, here in Statesville, who are the mighty fortresses of God, who have fought for the sake of faith and are moving on to perfection. It is the hope of many within the institutionalized resurrection community of the church that we will one day join them. But for now we struggle. We sing of the saints; we talk of the saints. But take heart, as the hymn says: "I sing a song of the saints of God . . . And I plan to be one, too!"

---

5. William Walsham How (1864).

BEING AT HOME IS A MINDSET OF FAITH

FALL 2011

Recently, I visited someone who kept saying she wanted to go home. This lady, who was very ill, yearned for the home she had known for so long. This home for her was a place where children were raised, where a marriage was cultivated to fruition, a harbor of hope, joy, and love. She yearned to be home. I knew in those moments that while she wanted to be in a place with a physical address and tangible elements, what she needed were the implications of being in that place.

We all deal with those emotions, don't we? This is a season of endings and beginnings for many. Students are heading back to schools in Iredell County, while other students are beginning their tenure at universities across the state and country. People are entering our community because of job opportunities or retirement, and the landscape of our time and place can change drastically from day to day. I often wonder if that's a symptom of a deeper problem. Many people lack a place to call home these days. People don't have the roots that the generation of yesterday had. I would argue that while people don't stay where they were planted, the roots matter more than ever.

We are a people built by our homes and the God who reigns over our homes. We are loved beyond measure by the people who represent the divine to us; that is why, deep down, all college students wish they could come home, why all parents strive to make life better for their children than what they had, and why those in their golden years hope for the simplicity they once knew in the homes of their youth. But in all those situations, we forget one important element. Home never left us. God has inspired a life in all of us that allows us to journey to the far reaches of the earth not only with the presence of our creator but also with the hopes, dreams, joys, and frustrations of that which we know as home. The reason all of us work for a home is that those moments when we are home, wherever that is, are moments in which God intricately weaves designs of holiness.

This week, be thankful for your homes. If your homes are changing for whatever reason, know that home is more than a building—home is a mindset. It is a mindset of grace that leads us to a deeper understanding of our faith in the midst of this transient life. Never be afraid to dream and wish for home, but be forever reminded that home is never too far from that dream or wish, for God is our home.

God is the surrounding presence that inspired those first feelings of belonging so long ago. Let us give thanks that no matter our reality, God is there, love is incarnate, and home is the mindset we can all work toward.

HOW WILL THEY REMEMBER YOU WHEN YOU'RE GONE?

OCTOBER 25, 2013

This past week, I conducted a celebration of life service at a beloved church I serve. The packed sanctuary was a reminder to all who were present of this church member's caring spirit. As we sat and heard stories from the family, one line stood out to me. One family member said, "She always wanted to remind us that we were never too old to dance in the kitchen."

The theologian Frederick Buechner writes this about remembering:

> When you remember me, it means you have carried something of who I am with you, that I have left some mark of who I am on who you are. It means that you can summon me back to your mind even though countless years and miles may stand between us. It means that if we meet again, you will know me. It means that even after I die, you can still see my face and hear my voice and speak to me in your heart.[6]

How do you want to be remembered?

Do you want to be called a memory over your accolades or wealth? Do you want to be remembered because you were the best at something, what ever that something might be? Or do you want to be recalled as someone who dances in the kitchen? Friends, our mark on this world is important.

---

6. *Listening to Your Life: Daily Meditations with Frederick Buechner*, comp. George Connor (San Francisco: Harper San Francisco, 1992), 14.

When we leave a place either by choice or death or other circumstances, we will be remembered. What do you want to commit to posterity?

The God who created us and loves us wants us to create memories and be a part of memories that make a difference in this world. It was Mother Teresa who said, "We can do no great things, only small things with great love." What might happen if that became our mindset in the creation of memories?

This week, challenge yourself to leave a legacy worthy of the love God has given you. I'm reminded of the words of an old camp song: "That's how it is with God's love, once you've experienced it, you spread the love to everyone, you want to pass it on." We are all called to pass on the legacy of grace and hope to everyone we come in contact with.

Most important, remember that you are a beloved part of God's creation and you will be remembered. Throughout the course of your daily life, continue to remember those people who have impacted you, those people who have given you permission to dance in the kitchen or sing while no one is around. For those people are the light of life and the hope of the resurrection of our souls and our memories. Take heart, people of God, for even when we dance in the kitchen, we are living out God's plan for our lives.

SAINTS, A REMINDER OF LIFE'S BEAUTY

NOVEMBER 1, 2013

Renowned writer and philosopher Fyodor Dostoevsky said it best: "The world will be saved by beauty."

Today is All Saints' Day, a time when the church marks the ineffable, indescribable connection we have to those who have gone before us. This holy day in the Christian year stands as a reminder of our connection to a vast canopy of saints and a world beyond what we know now. In a world so marred by ugliness and evil, it's wonderful to know that God is working through the beauty of the dead and the living.

This day is also one to remind us that saints were all normal people. They lived with grace and dignity; they valued human life and the beauty of diversity. From St. Luke to St. Genevieve to the friend or loved one who has just left this world, they all share a story that intertwines love, humility, and justice. God completed a work in them, and that is the consolation we have when someone joins the glorious company of the saints of light. It may not be easy or even make sense—in fact, it often doesn't. But God takes the very worldly institution of death and makes it out of this world with hope and resurrection.

I find it ever more appropriate that our world turns to fall as we mark All Saints' Day. Is it any coincidence that as leaves fall and die, they become bright reminders of beauty and a reminder of what once was? Perhaps that's the point. I can only guess, but for me that is a wonderful connection to sainthood, for in sainthood we see the beauty of what once was and the promises of community. Another person who has joined the cloud of witnesses said, "We have all known the long loneliness, and we have all found that the answer is community."

Friends, this week, cherish those memories of community and people whom you love but see no more. In those moments, remind yourself that you too will join the community of blessed rest, for we are all homeward bound. In our quest for home, we rise and fall in grace, and ultimately that's what makes us saints, a grace present all the days of our lives.

I'll leave you with this prayer that has kept me in line with the saints that I love. May it find a place in your heart as well:

O Lord,
support us all the day long of this troublous life,
until the shadows lengthen, and the evening comes,
and the busy world is hushed,
and the fever of life is over, and our work is done.
Then, Lord, in thy mercy,
grant us a safe lodging, a holy rest,
and peace at the last.
Amen.[7]

May you find comfort and strength in the saints, for they remind us of the light of life and the joy we all wish to know. In time, such beauty will save the world.

---

7. Prayer of Cardinal John Henry Newman (liturgyoffice.org.uk/Resources/OCF/Prayers-Time-Death.pdf).

WITH SPRING COMES NEW LIFE

MARCH 28, 2014

The other day, I was walking in my backyard with my dog when I came across a wildflower. I couldn't help but be encouraged by the beauty of the flower and its magnificence against the backdrop of the cold and dark winter we have experienced.

That got me thinking about one of my favorite hymns: "In the bulb there is a flower, in the seed an apple tree; in cocoons a hidden promise: butterflies will soon be free! In the cold and snow of winter, there's a spring that waits to be, unrevealed until its season, something God alone can see."[8]

As we journey this spring toward Easter, how are you preparing for the new life that comes with resurrection? I'm not talking about eternal resurrection but the resurrection that comes with each new day of life. How has God called you to new life every day of your life?

Perhaps this time of year you can find yourself breathing in the fresh, crisp air and finding once more the beauty of our planet Earth. You can see the wonder in God's creation as each year spring resurrects from winter. How are you preparing for that in your own life? We can look again to the hymn I mentioned above for the answer: "In our end is our beginning; in our time infinity; in our doubt there is believing; in our life eternity. In our death a resurrection; at the last a victory, unrevealed until its season, something God alone can see."

People of faith, know that there is nothing—neither height, nor depth, not anything in all creation—that can separate us from the love in Jesus Christ. There is nothing we can do that would prevent us from experiencing a spring in our own lives. So this week, as you journey about in the

---

8. Natalie Sleeth, "Hymn of Promise" (Carol Stream, IL: Hope Publishing Co., 1986).

spring weather, be mindful that God is at work bringing about wildflowers in your life. God is present and love is incarnate. That is the greatest good news anyone could ever offer us. Thanks be to God!

LOOKING FORWARD TO A FUTURE WITH HOPE

JUNE 13, 2014

My younger brother Scott graduates from high school tomorrow. Scott will attend the University of North Carolina School of the Arts in the fall. I'm excited for Scott and all that's in store for him. That got me thinking about the future we are all called to live into. The reality of our lives is that the future can be quite daunting and scary. There are times when we can't make heads or tails of things. But let me give you three points to look for in a future with God in mind.

1. God's future for us does not always match our future plans. We all have plans, but I've heard it said that if you want to make God laugh, tell him your plans. The reality is that what's in store for you and for me is a far greater part of the bigger picture than our own conceptions of the future.

2. This is a day of new beginnings. This is a time to make new what was old, make beautiful spaces where there are not-so-beautiful things in our lives. This is an opportunity for God to bring life where there was none, hope where hope was absent, and love where love has long been forgotten. That's the beauty of our Creator: God works and works for those who love him. There is beauty in that.

3. Finally, remember that you don't have to walk this road alone. There is hope in the incarnation of God that we don't ever have to go this journey toward the future alone. God is incarnational and works through the person of Jesus Christ. But also, God works to make us into incarnational beings as well. With our willingness to walk together on this journey, God can do anything in our lives.

This week, look forward to God's future with hope, joy, and peace. For it is in that mindset that we are made new and prepared for whatever life has in store.

FUNERALS RESTORE OUR FAITH

JULY 9, 2015

Ask any minister you know, and he or she will say that sometimes it's a funeral week.

I am either attending or officiating three funerals this week, and it can be quite the hectic time. Have you ever been to a really good funeral? How about a really bad funeral?

Funerals say a lot about people, and the church has a lot to say about funerals.

Here are some thoughts that I have during this week of going to and from funerals.

What we do at funerals matters. The chief purpose of a funeral is to proclaim Christ's resurrection from the dead and the resurrection offered to all of us. It is to celebrate the life of a person in the context of a worship service. It also is important to remember that the celebration of life is a narrative of the faith story of the person, so we tell the full story.

It's always interesting to go to funerals and hear the wonders and amazing things the deceased accomplished. Personally, I'd like to hear about how they fought struggles or faced the demons of life.

The narrative of faith is not always easy, fun, or happy, but it's something we all should hear. It's also important not to make a saint out of someone who struggled. That's God's job. God refines and defines who we are, so we must be honest about the struggles and hardships while celebrating the accomplishments and the joyful times.

Finally, I once read a This I Believe article titled "Always Go to the Funeral."

In the article, Deirdre Sullivan writes, "Always go to the funeral means that I have to do the right thing when I really, really don't feel like it."[9]

We all should go to the funerals of those around us, even if it's difficult. For, in so doing, we proclaim Christ as risen savior until he comes again in glory. We mark the passing of this life to the next, and that is a restorative act.

Truly, I believe we are all reminded of our salvation at funerals. We are reminded that in life, in death, and in life beyond death, we are not alone. That, my friends, is the most beautiful thing we could ever hope for. Thanks be to God for life, for death, and for life beyond death. Amen!

---

9. "Always Go to the Funeral," This I Believe series, on NPR's *All Things Considered*, August 8, 2005 (npr.org/2005/08/08/4785079/always-go-to-the-funeral).

IS THE CHURCH DYING?

FALL 2011

Church attendance is on the decline, and church membership is on a downward slope to nowhere. Where are we headed as a church? Many have said that we are headed to the dark abyss of history, that one day our children and grandchildren will reminisce about the days when their parents went to church. They, in turn, will be spending their Sunday mornings not in church, doing something else instead.

Church is no longer what it once was. We took advantage of the fact that the church was like food and water, or even the very air we breathe. We examined church as a necessity within society. The implications of this are grim. We now have a problem: it's like the church is running out of air. I'm sure you've all heard the phrase "dying breed." Well, the church is exactly that—on its way out.

I'm sure you didn't start reading this to hear about the grim reality that is the church's future. I didn't start writing it to convey that grim reality. We all must come to the table together and work towards the solution. It doesn't help any of us to talk about the death of the church, because it hasn't happened yet. We are still fighting the disease of apathy within the church. But we are still alive!

I have a minister friend in Charlotte by the name of Jim Trollinger. He is currently in a battle of his own. He is fighting stage 4 brain cancer. He keeps telling people that he is not a statistic or a textbook example of what happens when someone gets cancer; he is, in fact, very alive.

I don't know about you, but as a part of the church community, I am very much alive! I fight every day for justice, peace, and reconciliation within the community of faith and beyond. That is our mission, not to sit and whine about our eventual downfall but to make the years we have count. I went to see the movie *Super 8* not too long ago, and at one of the pivotal moments in that movie the protagonist declares in the midst of doom, "Bad things happen, but you can still live!" Church, you can have bad things happen to you, but you are still very much alive!

It is my challenge to you to take the future of our church into your own hands. Be like my friend Jim and fight the very fight of life! That is what we must do; that is what we are called to do. God is present in the midst of our struggle.

WHAT FOOD MEANS FOR RESURRECTION

MAY 19, 2016

The church I serve in Raleigh, North Carolina, just started our summer sermon series. We've titled it "Good Eats," and we're talking about all the famous biblical stories of breaking bread together. We're showing that meals were an important part of Scripture and important to the people of faith whose story Scripture tells. As I was preparing my sermon for my set Sunday, I started thinking about one particular meal that stood out to me as one I cherish, and it simply involved a bottle of Coke and some Twizzlers.

In high school I was involved with a leadership program in Statesville that took us on tours of various parts of city government, culture, and life. I remember hanging out with my high school friends and the joy it brought me. One particular day, though, I was incredibly bored. For whatever reason, I couldn't get involved with walking around and seeing artwork. So my friend Abbey and I did the unthinkable. We skipped and got Twizzlers and glass bottles of Coca-Cola. To make all of you educators happy and to head off any younger readers, we both were caught. But what joy and satisfaction I had in a shared meal with a friend.

You see, I count that experience as the last meal I had with Abbey before she passed on to what lies beyond this life. I cherish that meal as a snapshot of grace personified and love incarnate. How precious life is, and how precious breaking bread together can be if done in the spirit of love and grace.

It's hard to be mad at someone you break bread with. It's hard to ignore someone's story if you sit with them for a meal. So it's my challenge to you this summer to share a feast with someone you aren't used to sharing a meal with. I challenge you to share a meal with someone you don't particularly care for, and you will find fresh amounts of grace, love, and hope within the conversation and "story-linking" of our faith, as one theologian calls it.

I look back on my time sharing that meal with Abbey as one of the most cherished memories I have. I hope that in your time and place, your meals shared around the dinner table, or with a pack of Twizzlers and a bottled Coke, can be a holy and magnificent moment. I hope you will consider your own good eats, those snapshots of shared fellowship and food that bring you close to the heart of God.

LEAVE SPACE FOR TRANSITION

DECEMBER 8, 2016

There is so much going on in my life right now. I know that's a cliché for many people these days. We spend our lives going from here to there and back again. We've made a business of transitioning from one part of life to the next. From cradle to grave, we're always having milestones of change and transition. But I'm starting to think we've gotten this wrong. We spend our entire lives trying to get somewhere. Perhaps this holiday season we can appreciate the transitional moments of life.

Perhaps you have a job offer on the table nagging at you, or you have a major surgery coming up. Perhaps you're getting married, or you've spent your entire life trying to get somewhere only to realize that wasn't the place you wanted to be. Naturally, we want to fix things, we want to accept or decline a particular offer, we want the surgery to happen, we want the wedding date to arrive, and we want the place where we are to be the place where we want to be. I'm saying all of this because in these Advent moments, I've been fixated this year on the Blessed Virgin Mary.

When Mary said "yes" to the angel Gabriel in Galilee, she had to wait nine grueling months before the nativity of our Lord Jesus Christ. Her yes to God's call took time, effort, and was no doubt painstakingly hard for her. We crunch all this together at Christmastime, but I think that makes my message today even more appropriate: we need to leave space for transition.

Leave room for the "what ifs" in life. Leave room and space for the middle moments of our existence. We may not be there yet, and that's okay. We must cherish the moment, for it is fleeting. We must be like Mary and, with our answer to God's call, realize the implications and transitions involved in what must come to pass.

If I've learned anything this past year, it's that hope is found in the middle, in that space between where we've come from and where we're meant to be. May we be bold in our acceptance of transition and seek peace in the midst of it. I can't solve all the problems we face, but I know someone who can: a person born in first-century Palestine who came and lived among us in the nitty-gritty of life. If Christmas means anything to you, let it be that there is space for God's unfolding future in your life and in the life of the world. God is not done yet, and in that transitional state of "not yet," let's find God there—working, restoring, and redeeming.

TO DEAR OLE DUKE, WITH LOVE

MAY 4, 2017

I finished my coursework for my master of theological studies degree at Duke University Divinity School on Tuesday. I have my degree conferred on May 13 at Duke University Chapel, and I wanted to take this moment to reflect on some of the most formative years of my educational career in the hopes that you all might glean something from what I've learned here in the land of the Blue Devils.

1. Never underestimate the beauty of fresh air. I spent six days in the hospital during my first year at Duke, and I hope never to take for granted the beauty of God's created order.

2. In the end, your GPA won't get you into heaven, nor will degrees conferred or accolades earned. What will get you there is a steadfast relationship with God and active participation in what God is doing in the world.

3. Take care to smell the roses. Two years at Duke have flown by, and frankly I find myself touching the walls and windows in the hopes of not missing anything that I could have possibly missed in my two years here.

4. Be prepared for roadblocks and course changes. The only constant in life is change, and we are forced to reckon with it. But the God we know and serve comes to us and reassures us in that change that God is still God.

5. Never ever take for granted the friends you've made along the way. To Palmer, Kelli, Patrick(s), and countless others, I am so grateful that you were my network of friendship in this place.

6. If all else fails, find a family and fiancée who will support you, even if you call in the middle of the night in tears because you may have failed your ethics exam.

7. Be committed to lifelong learning. I'm already looking at doctor of ministry programs.

8. Be thankful for the saints who influenced you but are cheering you on from across the Jordan. What I would give to have my great-grandparents (Wilma, Robert, and Nonnie Fay) or my friend Abbey Tsumas here to celebrate my graduation. But alas, I know they are watching from a distance with great expectations.

9. Keep the faith. God is not done with you yet. God will never leave you nor forsake you. That is a great and certain hope that we have as people of faith.

10. Never be afraid to sail away from safe harbor and risk something big for something good. I feel that pretty much sums it up.

Dear ole Duke, you have been kind to me. You have challenged me. You have brought me to a place of faith and higher learning I never thought possible. As I leave the halls of this seminary, as I go forth to do God's work in the world, I know I take these and countless other lessons with me. May we be bold in our resolve to learn and to love. That is the heart of the good news.

DOUG EASON'S FAITH LEGACY

JULY 13, 2017

Doug Eason was a friend with whom I could always find conversation. His life was a witness to the beauty of education. Whenever I visited with him, whether in the pews of our beloved Broad Street United Methodist Church or in his home, I knew I would always enjoy a rousing conversation on theology, the great novels of eras gone by, or his trips with his beloved wife. He had impeccable penmanship, and I consider myself lucky to have received a few handwritten notes from the man who steered Mitchell Community College for years. He died Wednesday.

Here's where I messed up with Doug, though: toward the end of his life he couldn't get out much, and I knew it was important that I go see him; I just never found the time. I never found an appropriate place in my schedule for a visit with Dr. Eason as his health declined. So, when I learned of his death, I learned the tough lesson we all must learn: time matters to God.

God, in God's infinite beauty, gave us time to sit with one another and enjoy each other's company.

The ultimate test for us is, will we take advantage of this? The ultimate test for us is, will we make time for one another in the finite moments we have? I know I may have failed to see Doug before his death, but I take consolation in a theologian he and I would speak of, the late Marcus Borg. Borg said this about death: "So, is there an afterlife, and if so, what will it be like? I don't have a clue. But I am confident that the one who has buoyed us up in life will also buoy us up through death. We die into God. What more that means, I do not know. But that is all I need to know."[10]

We all die into the love and grace of God. We all go home. I give thanks for the life and witness of Dr. Doug Eason, who taught me many things, most importantly that time matters to us and to God.

Well done, good and faithful servant.

---

10. Marcus Borg, *Speaking Christian: Why Christian Words Have Lost Their Meaning and Power—And How They Can Be Restored* (New York: HarperOne, 2011), 201.

LIVE LIFE IN GOD'S TIME

APRIL 2015

These past few weeks have flown by for me, and I think I know why. This Sunday, I was ordained to Christian ministry by the church I serve. Next week, I will graduate from Appalachian State University with a Bachelor of Arts in religious studies. It is exciting, humbling, and surreal at the same time.

There are many twists and turns that have led me to this place, and I've been waiting for this moment for some time.

"Enjoy these moments. Your life will forever change on Sunday. It's a whirlwind," said one of the clergy who participated in the service.

In Christian Wiman's book, *My Bright Abyss: Meditation of a Modern Believer*, he writes, "The greatest tragedy of human existence is not to live in time, in both senses of that phrase." As created beings of a loving and living God, we are called to live in our time and our place. We were created to be people who love the time we've been given.

That means we should be cherishing the present, even when it's hard to do. We spend our lives looking forward to things—in my case, my ordination and my graduation. But in so doing, we forget to smell the beautiful roses God created. So this week, take time to breathe and enjoy everything that God has for you in this time and place.

As we go through our time on this Earth, let us live in time, being sure to remember that the greatest time we have is right now in the present. Let God work with your present situation to make it beautiful. In so doing, God will complete a good work in you.

I'm still really excited for the next few weeks too, culminating with my graduation, but I'm trying hard to enjoy the days leading up to the pinnacle and whirlwind of my college career. For as it was with Elijah, God wasn't in the fire or the earthquake moments; God was in the stillness of time and space, so look for those moments and find grace there (1 Kgs 19, NRSV).

AN INTERVIEW WITH DR. STANLEY HAUERWAS

FALL 2011

Author's note: As a young student of theology I always looked up to Dr. Stanley Hauerwas, an esteemed professor at Duke Divinity School. After completing a course of study at Duke during high school, I asked to interview Dr. Hauerwas for the newspaper. Here is our conversation.

Question: Dr. Hauerwas, in one of your pieces, "The Ethicist as Theologian," you speak of humor being important to theological reflection. How do you feel about the issue of theology and humor? How do they coexist?
Stanley Hauerwas: These are good questions, by the way. The relation between theology and humor is very simple: what could be more humorous than theologians thinking they can say something interesting about God? God surely laughs at our efforts. I think it's probably true that you shouldn't trust a theologian who doesn't have a good sense of humor. Theology and humor must coexist.

Q: *How has the church embarrassed you in your beliefs? We all find times when we cringe at what the church has done. How does that pertain to your personal walk of faith?*
SH: I'm not sure I've thought of the church embarrassing my beliefs. But I often worry if I embarrass faithful Christians. I do, of course, worry about the accommodated character of the church. But in that same accommodated church I often discover lives that put my own life in perspective. So God is great, able to raise up faithful Christians even in the midst of a severely compromised church.

Q: How can a person or church in a small town truthfully hold fast to theological ethics within the context of the greater community?
SH: Well, smallness doesn't necessarily mean "narrow." It can mean locality which allows for the development of practical reason and judgment that cannot be known elsewhere. So I say, take advantage of locality.

Q: At Duke, you teach a course on John Howard Yoder's The Politics of Jesus. Yoder's work is phenomenal and lays claim to Jesus' response to the social behavior of his disciples. How do you think that Jesus would respond to the social behavior of modern-day Christians?
SH: I suspect Jesus would think that those who call ourselves Christians are pretty close to those he identifies in the Gospel of Matthew as scribes and Pharisees. It's a harsh judgment, but it's one I fear is unavoidable.

Q: Finally, Dr. Hauerwas, death and dying seem to be on the headlines of news these days. Society is fascinated by it, but how should the church respond to the issues of death and dying? I know you have done significant research in this as an issue of ethical behavior, and I hope this isn't too forward, but how do you see death coming for you? How can a Christian live a life ready for death?
SH: I'm not sure if Christians today can live lives such that they are ready to die. We simply no longer know how to do that. We can, however, keep before us that we are a people shaped by martyrdom. That can never be forgotten. Just to the extent that we remember this, we continue to have hope that we too will be faithful as we face death.

LOVE IS THE WAY HOME

JANUARY 31, 2019

Never have I written such a pressing column. Never have I committed pen to paper the way I have now. You may have heard I had a seizure this week and almost lost my life after I stopped breathing. Eyewitness accounts say I turned blue and lost a pulse, so two brave App State students administered CPR. In the twilight moments between life and death, I saw something. Now, before you turn the page of the paper or click away and think this is another "Come and find Jesus" moment, I implore you to trust me and your best angels and hear me out.

I saw my late Uncle John and my late friend Abbey. I saw them as clearly as I could see them the day they died, and I heard messages of resilience and hope. I've made a conscious decision to keep some of these messages to myself, not to torture you, but in the sure and certain hope that I can live out these moments in this sphere.

You see, I went to Duke University, one of the finest research institutions in the nation. I have trained with some of the best theologians and held conversations with powerful people. So every time I heard about one of these "near death" experiences, I explained them away as a lack of oxygen and an opportunity for ten seconds of fame.

But then life ends, even if but for a minute, and suddenly all of that doesn't matter. My master of theological studies didn't stop my seizure; the best theologians couldn't explain what I saw in that moment in the hereafter. Don't get me wrong: I still am filled with doubt about many things. But what I am confident in more than ever is that this life matters to God.

I beg you to make life count. I beg you to make life matter for others. My whole life has been in the pursuit of God's abiding love, and this week I experienced it in weird and dynamic ways. But in seeing a long-dead uncle and friend, I have felt my faith restored. I have felt my life find purpose again. The love that has endured in my story will continue to endure because that love made me and will bring me home.

So here's what you can take away: I don't have time for the typical Statesville platitudes anymore, and you shouldn't either. Love deeply, fiercely, and remarkably. Do so without regard to the cost or what your church or city council might say. Do what makes you happy and love the skin that you inhabit. Love others and show that love is the most powerful force in the world. Show someone they're worth living for, because in the end, we're walking each other home.

I love you all. Thank you for reading this column these past eight years, and thank you for believing in me. Let's keep writing and exploring the amazing love of God.

DO ALL DOGS GO TO HEAVEN?

SUMMER 2018

In April 1899, Mark Twain wrote to a friend, "The dog is a gentleman; I hope to go to his heaven, not man's."

After years of studying theology, I seem to be carrying a lot of theological weight around the subject of the soteriology (a theological word for salvation) of animals. The other day, someone on Twitter referred to me as an advocate for the salvation of animals, and I couldn't have been prouder.

The same day, one of my favorite radio personalities, NPR's Lulu Garcia-Navarro, was asking how to respond to the mortality of a fish when speaking with a child. I hope this helps, because we're all wondering what it means when our beloved pet passes away.

For me, it's been a recent personal question: Did my guinea pig Cleopas make it to the pearly gates? And what does the answer to that question say about God?

I want to preface my answer to these questions by saying the church militant is not of one accord on these issues. Until recently, the Roman Catholic Church, for instance, did not subscribe to the idea that animals will reach paradise, because they do not have souls. That was until Pope Francis said, "Eternal life will be a shared experience of awe, in which each creature, resplendently transfigured, will take its rightful place and have something to give these poor men and women who will have been liberated once and for all."[11]

---

11. Encyclical Letter, Laudato Sí, Of the Holy Father, Francis, On Care for Our Common Home, IX. Beyond the Sun, §243 (vatican.va/content/francesco/en/encyclicals/documents/papa-francesco_20150524_enciclica-laudato-si.html).

John Wesley, an eighteenth-century Anglican priest and founder of the Methodist tradition, preached a sermon titled "The General Deliverance" in which he proclaimed that since animals were not responsible for the planet, they would receive ample rewards for their "present sufferings."[12]

What Wesley and Francis are saying gets to the heart of a loving and liberating God. We will all be changed by eternity's light. If we are loved by God in this life, how much more the delight will be in the world to come, whatever that looks like. We are enveloped in love in this life, and this is coming for us in the next life. We are loved no matter where we come from or where we're going. We are loved because God loves creation, and I'm sure the heart of God breaks when we don't care for our surroundings and furry friends.

Though I will not speculate on what karat of gold the streets might be in heaven, nor will I say that I'm even certain of what's to come, I will say that, where God is, one day all my pets will join their place in the angel choir. That goes for Cleopas the guinea pig and, yes, Lulu Garcia-Navarro's pet fish too.

As Ram Dass famously said, "We're all just walking each other home."

---

12. Wesley Center Online, "The General Deliverance," Sermon 60, II:9 (wesley.nnu.edu/john-wesley/the-sermons-of-john-wesley-1872-edition/sermon-60-the-general-deliverance/).

CONVERSATIONS CAN CHANGE PERSPECTIVES

JANUARY 24, 2014

This past week I was in San Francisco, researching and working in a church in that community that specializes in work with marginalized people, including the increasingly growing homeless population.

One day, my research partner and I signed up to work at a soup kitchen at the church to get on-the-ground experience in the community. While I wasn't the most excited about this endeavor, I was nonetheless blessed and humbled by a lady named Pat.

You see, San Francisco, California, is a completely different place from Statesville, North Carolina. While we with Southern sensibilities view saying "Yes ma'am" as a normal means of politeness ingrained in us by our parents since birth, the people on the West Coast view that phrase as odd and out of place. So in the course of my conversation with Pat, a homeless lady who roams the streets of San Francisco, I referred to her as "ma'am," and she was surprised. She looked at me and said, "No one has referred to me as 'ma'am' since before I was homeless. Thank you for that blessing."

Conversations that have the simple appearance of a daily routine have the potential to bring about blessings for both parties. Isn't it amazing how God works through words like "yes ma'am" to bring about a blessing for Pat and a lesson in grace for me? We are challenged to be a part of the loving work of God in conversational grace.

This week, examine how your conversations might find God intertwined within them. It may be at the grocery store checkout counter, Fifth Street Ministries, or the hospital. Ultimately, God is working everywhere, so find yourself lost in the beauty of God in conversation.

Finally, my friend Theon, the associate pastor at the church where I was researching, gave a benediction at church on Sunday that challenged us to be "doers of grace." May we be so bold as to be doers and hearers. May we be full of kindness, love, and hope in a conversation that might be life changing. May we find ourselves lost in the mystery of human interaction and the hope of God showing up in that interaction. For that is where grace happens.

ON THE EVE OF SOMETHING GLORIOUS: TO STEPHANIE'S GRANDMOTHER

FEBRUARY 14, 2019

Gram,

    You never needed to know the "why" of my wife and me. The first time you met me you said you prayed that "I would be the one for Stephanie." I thank you for that prayer. Now that you've witnessed a Thanksgiving you wanted to see and the New England Patriots continue their Super Bowl legacy this year, it's my turn to pray for you. You are about to start the journey of the hereafter, and I am about to leave to visit you soon. This may very well be the last time I see you, so I wanted to let you know a few things about the next part of your grand adventure.

    You may be scared, you may be frightened of what's next and what is to come. Let me assure you that the same God who was present at your first breath will be there at your last. I know that may not be as comforting as it sounds, and let me be the first to say I think this sucks. But I also know that the God you and I talked about late into the night will be there for you, and that same God will be there for my wife, for me, for her entire family. So be at peace there; we will hold your memory forever, and we will cherish it.

    I will cherish what you said when I married the love of my life. I will never forget the day I graduated from seminary and you made me get my academic regalia on when I was with you so you could see it. The day I resigned my church position, you were ready to drive to that church even though you hadn't driven in years. This is the hope I have of keeping your love and light alive. You have shown me the heart of God, so I know where Stephanie gets that talent.

Gram, I don't want to speculate about the streets and the pearly gates. You will see whatever is next soon. But I know your husband will be there, I know that all the saints you have faithfully prayed with and to will be there, and I know that one day we all will join you and you will be waiting for us.

One of my wife's favorite memories is singing karaoke to you last Thanksgiving. You have changed lives, so take comfort there. You have shown so many that love will overcome the worst of our fears. Please keep us close. Please keep us safe. Please let the Virgin Mary know that Protestants like me don't appreciate her enough. Most important, feel safe in the loving arms of God.

We will see you on the other side of the Jordan. It feels like this ending is the end of it all. But I refuse to believe that a soul as beautiful as yours is done. You are going on to glory, so be at peace, and may light perpetual shine upon you.

With Love,
Rob

MOMENTS THAT DEFINED A JOURNEY

No one needs to tell me about the importance of the free press in a democratic society or about the essential role a newspaper can play in its community.
—Robert F. Kennedy (from "Address to the American Society of Newspaper Editors," April 28, 1961)

These columns are providential because they showed me the heart of a living and loving God. Now, that isn't to say they're all butterflies and daisies. Indeed, some of them are gut-wrenching. But I have found that God is showing up in all of these, and God is never finished, despite our feeble attempt to end the sentence.

FRIENDSHIP AND FAITH ARE IMPORTANT TO GOD

FEBRUARY 8, 2019

My friend Ruwa is one of my absolute favorite people. She is kind, she is intelligent, and she and her husband always give me a place to stay when I'm doing doctoral research and work in Washington, DC, but I'm starting to think after reading the comment section of this newspaper that she wouldn't be welcomed here by some in this town.

Ruwa is one of the most faithful people I know. That's not what would give you pause or cause you to stare. She faithfully asks deep questions of our existence, volunteers, and is politically active. Ruwa is also a person of the Muslim faith. Sure, we poke fun at each other for me being an ordained Christian pastor and Ruwa being active in her religious community, but the question has long plagued me: Will I have to spend the hereafter without her? Is her faith and its beauty beyond the grace of what the Christian faith can offer or, dare I say, vice versa?

I want to propose that the greatest gift God has given me is people like Ruwa, people who don't share the same faith as me. To suggest that heaven is perfected without her doesn't sound very heavenly to me. Now I know the Scripture that will be thrown at me, but luckily Scripture isn't my only source of understanding.

I was raised Wesleyan, and we believe not only Scripture as a basis of our faith but also tradition, reason, and experience (also called the Wesleyan Quadrilateral). This understanding of how God works in the world leads me to believe that the answer of our existence is far greater than denominational or religious identity.

To suggest that somehow my experience of what God does in the world is more than Ruwa's is shallow and sad. To say I will be rewarded for my faith and she won't is downright ridiculous. We have pieces of the puzzle, not the whole set. So the question becomes, in a place filled with half-truths, would we look at Ruwa with judgment, or would we look at her with love and friendship?

I believe even more after coming close to death that all things on Earth grow strangely dim in the light of God's glory and grace: all things, our political beliefs, our religious theologies, and our understanding of what matters.[13] When I was in the hospital, I wasn't praying the sinner's prayer; I was hoping I'd get to see strong figures in my life like mom, Stephanie, and Ruwa. I wasn't making amends with God; I was reckoning with what I had left undone here, like visiting people more often. That's because God cares deeply about how we love down here. God cares that we love not for conversion, but for the sanctification of the whole human family. So, Statesville, it looks like God cares—do you?

---

13. See Helen Howarth Lemmel, "Turn Your Eyes upon Jesus" (1922).

THOUGHTS ON WORLD SUICIDE PREVENTION DAY

SEPTEMBER 2014

I remember it like it was yesterday: the day after my uncle committed suicide. My little brother got in the car with me at after-school pickup and announced that Uncle John was in hell because he committed suicide. When Mom asked where in the hell he got that from, Scott replied that a teacher at our private Christian school had told him so. I credit that day with being the day my theological wheels started turning. I wanted nothing to do with a god who would condemn his child, our beloved John, to hell because of John's illness and an action he took against himself. Little did I know that I too would face the reality of suicide personally.

There are some things in life that have been deemed unavoidable, such as taxes and death. Unfortunately, some of us wish death to come by our own means and ways. We are in such a dark position and place that nothing can break into the darkness. No person or prayer can keep people from that darkness. And some of us wear the scars of suicide attempts either physically or mentally. Some of us succeed and die far too soon.

So on this World Suicide Prevention Day, I want to remind you of the words of Scripture that I have come to know for myself. Romans 8 has this to say:

> What then are we to say about these things? If God is for us, who is against us? He who did not withhold his own Son, but gave him up for all of us, will he not with him also give us everything else? Who will bring any charge against God's elect? It is God who

justifies. Who is to condemn? It is Christ Jesus, who died, yes, who was raised, who is at the right hand of God, who indeed intercedes for us. Who will separate us from the love of Christ? Will hardship, or distress, or persecution, or famine, or nakedness, or peril, or sword? As it is written, "For your sake we are being killed all day long; we are accounted as sheep to be slaughtered." No, in all these things we are more than conquerors through him who loved us. For I am convinced that neither death, nor life, nor angels, nor rulers, nor things present, nor things to come, nor powers, nor height, nor depth, nor anything else in all creation, will be able to separate us from the love of God in Christ Jesus our Lord. (Rom 8:31-39, NRSV)

There is nothing, no one, no principality or power that can keep us from God's love. If you are facing the dark abyss of suicide, know that God stands with you and is for you. God gave us tools to face these realities—friends, family, clergy, psychologists, and psychiatrists—so use them to the best of your ability and fight the situation you are in. And when it seems like you can't fight anymore, lean into God and your support system to live on and live fully. This is easier said than done, of course. But God is bigger than what we face, and we have the capacity to fight the dark reality of suicide.

St. Francis De Sales (1567–1622) has this prayer I offer up today:

Be at peace.
Do not look forward in fear to the changes of life;
rather look to them with full hope as they arise.
God, whose very own you are, will deliver you from out of them.
He has kept you hitherto, and He will lead you safely through all
   things;
and when you cannot stand it, God will bury you in His arms.
Do not fear what may happen tomorrow;
the same everlasting God who cares for you today
will take care of you then and every day.
God will either shield you from suffering, or will give you unfailing
   strength to bear it.
Be at peace, and put aside all anxious thoughts and imagination.[14]

---

14. Prayer of St. Francis De Sales, stfrancislzparish.org/patron-saint.

I wish I could have one more conversation with my Uncle John, someone who over the course of my life I've come to admire and adore. Though he was sick, he knows what I've gone through and I wish he had the resources I now have to fight the dying of the light. But perhaps John's legacy and my legacy can offer some vulnerability about this issue. I am a person who has faced suicide, and I know that through reaching out to my resources I have fought back, and you can too. So take heart, keep the faith, and never ever, ever, ever forget that you are loved.

SHABBAT SHALOM, Y'ALL

OCTOBER 7, 2017

I had the opportunity to speak at Anshe Emet Synagogue in the heart of Wrigleyville in Chicago last night. The experience was nothing short of redemptive, and here's why: As I was being introduced, I felt the anxiety I deal with rising. Would I say something wrong? Would I offend a community I have such respect for? Would they respond well to what I had to say about my experiences as a Southern person of faith?

All these thoughts were racing through my head until Rabbi Michael Siegel, the senior rabbi of the synagogue, rose to introduce me. He spoke in Hebrew at first, and I quickly recalled my seminary work in trying to learn Hebrew, but he took pity on me and explained: in the Jewish tradition, when there are no leaders, God raises up leaders to speak as God did with the prophets.

I took my place and delivered my thoughts on Ezekiel and the dry bones. I offered the liberating word that had been offered to me by God to them and encouraged them to speak up and speak out in the name of the God we worship. Then, after the service, we went and feasted on a traditional Jewish meal for the festival of Sukkot, a festival immediately following Yom Kippur.

We laughed, we made jokes about the Philadelphia Eagles to the resident Eagles fan, and we drank bourbon and whiskey that was the strongest I've ever had. We celebrated the common bonds of friendship, of kindness, of faith, and of fellowship. I was extended hospitality I would never receive in most mainline churches.

Rabbi Siegel and I spoke of the hope we had for our respective institutions. We laughed over the commonality of my favorite movie *Keeping the Faith* (2001), and we lamented the state of our country. In their magnificent synagogue, they had a stained-glass window that was etched with the passage from Genesis that said God created us in God's image and then with that famous American line, "All men are created equal." I will never forget that Rabbi Siegel looked at me and said, "We still have work to do."

I couldn't agree more: we still have work to do, yet today I celebrate the common bonds of faith that brought me to Anshe Emet Synagogue in the first place. Though this has been an eventful month in my life, I found new beginnings last night as my hosts Marsha and Brian took me with their children to Wrigley Field. (The Cubs won, by the way, so I'm now a good luck charm to them!)

One of the most important things I experienced was the repetition of the Jewish faith. They repeated God's deeds of power in their lives and in the life of their community. Though I had to work to keep up with the Hebrew, I knew that they were worshiping the living and loving God I serve as well. Deeper than that, during their repetitions they were called to remember where they came from and ultimately where they were headed—toward wholeness and completion in their beautiful faith.

My message in the repetition of my story is simple: as Rabbi Siegel said, "When there are no leaders, God raises up leaders to speak as God did with the prophets." May we be bold in our resolve to be raised up as leaders in this country where our leaders are failing us. May we show hospitality to the stranger in our midst. Who knows? We might be entertaining Elijah or angels. This is our common bond, and this is our common hope.

REMEMBER YOUR BAPTISM AND BE THANKFUL

AUGUST 2014

This past weekend was a wonderful reminder of one of the most important acts the church participates in. I was at the North Carolina Aquarium at Fort Fischer. I saw Carolina Beach in the beauty of summer brilliance and closed the day with a walk along the Neuse River. This time spent with special people culminated on Sunday morning when the church I serve in the mountains baptized three people into the life of faith.

These instances reminded me of the 1992 Robert Redford film *A River Runs through It*, based on the book by Norman Maclean. This movie is set in small-town Montana, where two very different sons of a Presbyterian minister come of age during Prohibition-era America. In the movie, one of the sons, Norman, finally realizes as he's fly-fishing on the Blackfoot River that

> Eventually, all things merge into one, and a river runs through it. The river was cut by the world's great flood and runs over rocks from the basement of time. On some of those rocks are timeless raindrops. Under the rocks are the words, and some of the words are theirs.
>
> I am haunted by waters.[15]

---

15. Norman Maclean, *A River Runs through It and Other Stories* (Chicago: University of Chicago Press, 1976), 104.

In one of the greatest acts of holy mischief, the church takes an element consigned to destruction, despair, and utter terror and pours it on someone or immerses someone to the point at which God cannot be taken from them. They are God's beloved. They are then sent out, possibly to a wilderness or to a temple to turn over tables and change the world. Throughout the story of our faith, water has changed everything. From the flood in Genesis to the river of life in Revelation, we see our lives intertwined with this life-giving force.

Friends, remember your baptism. Remember your initiation and calling into the wonderful community of faith that you now call home. Kindle anew the Spirit that led yourself or your parents up to the altar for baptism. Celebrate that grace at work in your life whether you knew it was there or not.

But be careful: often we'd like it if baptism was the only way in which we could express our faith. But the God of our baptism calls us out of the waters and to take up a cross. Baptism is the beginning of something beautiful, something miraculous, but it is only the beginning.

This week, remember that our lives are haunted by water, for God is found in the water. God will do whatever it takes to reach us, racing through every street in every town, hamlet, and city until we find ourselves lost in the beauty of the waters of life. Our lives are haunted by water, and that's the best reality anyone could ever have.

WORKING TOGETHER IS A SIGN OF GOD'S KINGDOM

JANUARY 11, 2019

The other day, I had the privilege of meeting Rep. Alexandria Ocasio-Cortez in Washington, DC, while I'm here working on my doctoral program. I recognize that merely uttering her name in such a "purple" town like Statesville can cause consternation from both the right and the left. She has galvanized politics in a way that is signaling a new generation of political leaders is on the rise.

Then, at dinner, I sat with my friend and theological scholar Diana Butler Bass and her husband, Richard. We talked of the world in which we live and the hope we desperately need. Diana is older than me and of a different generation, but we share the same hopes and dreams for a better, more equitable world.

I tell you these two stories to show that it is going to take all of us to get to the point where we can fix this mess. It is going to take the younger and the older, the rich and the poor, the Republican and the Democrat, those of different races, orientations, and gender identities. It's going to take everyone.

Now you may say, "Preacher, that's not how this works. That's not how any of this works." But when I look to Jesus, the pioneer and perfecter of our faith (Heb 12:2), he surrounded himself with a motley crew to usher in the kingdom and reign of God. For that to happen again, we must remember that it's going to take all of God's children to bring about the reign and realm of God.

On Good Friday in 1963, the Reverend Dr. Martin Luther King Jr. wrote his "Letter from Birmingham Jail" after white clergymen in the area wrote to him asking for civility and a modest approach to integration. King wrote,

[T]he judgment of God is upon the church as never before. If today's church does not recapture the sacrificial spirit of the early church, it will lose its authenticity, forfeit the loyalty of millions, and be dismissed as an irrelevant social club with no meaning for the twentieth century. Every day I meet young people whose disappointment with the church has turned into outright disgust.

I want to echo King: if people of faith don't get it together, we're going to miss the point of why we have church in the first place. If we're so focused on keeping prayer in schools, we'll forget that God never left schools at all. If we're so focused on our own churches, we forget that Sunday is the most segregated hour of our week. If we're so focused on keeping our guns, we'll forget that one day in God's kingdom we will have no need for such things. We're so focused on locking up criminals that we forget them once they're in jail. We're so focused on building a wall that we forget that the wall is costing Americans their livelihoods and paychecks.

This very point is found in Jesus' first public sermon: "The Spirit of the Lord is upon me, because he has anointed me to bring good news to the poor. He has sent me to proclaim release to the captives and recovery of sight to the blind, to let the oppressed go free, to proclaim the year of the Lord's favor" (Luke 4:18-19).

We have work to do, and it's going to take everyone from the most fastidious conservative to the most ardent liberal to get it done. We can and must be better. For the sake of our children and our children's children, we have work to do.

THOUGH MUCH IS TAKEN, MUCH ABIDES

JANUARY 18, 2019

After last week's article, I was ready to hand in my pen and give up on writing articles for the paper. After a sincere call for unity and prayer for a better tomorrow, I received a death threat from someone who read the article and disagreed with my meeting with Rep. Alexandria Ocasio-Cortez. I'd like to publicly thank the Statesville Police Department and Councilman William Morgan for their amazing response.

Throughout this past week, I've fixated on Alfred Lord Tennyson's words, "Tho' much is taken, much abides."[16] I also received a call from my friend Anne, someone I haven't heard from in years. We laughed and I found myself in tears, but most important, we both agreed on something, a line from the show *Madam Secretary* that spoke to us: "To keep fighting the good fight in this line of work you have to have a big heart. Because it's constantly being chipped away at."

We need big-hearted people willing to abide in the mess of this life. This life is broken and beautiful. There is much to bemoan and there is much to engage in as we work for the day of our Lord Jesus Christ. I look to Dr. King, whose life we celebrate this weekend, and see that though he was taken from this world in the most violent of ways, we still have the legacy that abides in his story. Though we may disagree in this town, we can live out the cherished vision and dream of Martin Luther King Jr., who had the fortitude to believe that things can and must be better. He knew that, though the road was tough, we could reach the mountaintop.

---

16. Tennyson, "Ulysses," in *Victorian Poetry and Poetics*, 2nd ed. (Boston: Houghton Mifflin Co., 1959), p. 32, line 65.

I don't just commit these words to paper as platitudes or half-truths. None of us have time for half-truths in Statesville. Just like my friend Anne watching *Madam Secretary*, we have to be big-hearted people, people willing to be small enough to change and big enough for patience. We must change. We must be better. Our town depends on it.

EMBODY FAITH THIS SEASON

DECEMBER 6, 2013

For me, Bertha Hamilton is the embodiment of faith and a close mentor who has helped shape my life. She's a longtime employee of Iredell Memorial Hospital, and I sat down with her to talk about faith and how she experiences God.

"When I see the fall season that we come out of, and that everything will soon be springtime again, it's encouraging to see that happen in my own life and the lives of others," Hamilton said. "God continues to strengthen me and allows me to help other people; what he does through me allows me to encourage others."

Hamilton is always ready to help. She's a longtime member of Clark's Chapel Baptist Church and is assured that God will see us all through life's challenges and tribulations.

"I know that God is able to get us through anything," she said. "One thing I know is that whatever storms we go through, God is there when we go into those storms, when we are in the midst of those storms, and when we come out the other side."

As I pondered those words, I thought of this Advent season, this season when we expect all that Christmas will bring. When Hamilton embodies faith and love for me, she takes part in the divine plan of incarnation. We are all little incarnations of the Christmas story; we are all an incredible piece of an amazing puzzle. When we become like Christ, when we work toward being lost in wonder, love, and praise of our creator, we take part in the Christmas story.

When I asked Hamilton why she likes helping people so much, her response was simple: "I just do. It's what I do." However, in that answer, she gives voice to our hopes and dreams for this season.

We're all so consumed with the hustle and moving-about of this season that we forget we are called to be the people who simply "do." We are called to do ministry in the world, we are called to do the things that matter this time of year, to prioritize and realize that God calls us to serve and embody faith.

This week, may you be found simply "doing" faith. May you be found with the people like Hamilton, the unsung heroes of life who continue to embody an incarnation that happened so long ago, because that is when Christmas will happen. That is where we meet Jesus. Keep on searching. Christ is here in our midst; we just have to be open to seeing him.

THE PRECARIOUS POSITION OF CHURCH

JANUARY 2014

I've heard an enormous amount of chatter lately about the so-called "moral decline of America." Many people of various religious persuasions are convinced that our nation is headed toward a state of immorality and decline. One example is the debate in the Boy Scout organization regarding gay scouts. On one end of the spectrum, you have a group of people who ardently believe that Boy Scouting has lost its moorings and is forsaking its oath and law. They are convinced that they are right. On the other end, you have a group of people who believe that Boy Scouting is affirming its identity and oath by allowing gay scouts. They believe they are right. What complicates matters is that most of the people having this argument are Christians. So the question becomes, have we lost our way?

I think the answer to what is going on here is far more complex than any of us are willing to admit. We live in a polarizing dichotomy that encourages words like "them" and "us," and beyond that there is a tendency to determine our personal feelings as Divine will or inspiration. We all must be careful with these realities. To suggest that any of us know the heart and mind of God is to suggest that we have a monopoly on the wisdom of the ages and of our Creator. We must also be careful to shake our heads at the moral decline of America without looking at the church as a possible conduit for this decline to occur.

The church is in a precarious position. There are those among us who address theo-political issues liberally and those who address them conservatively. I use Boy Scouting as an example, but there are myriad other situations in which this is true. To be true to ourselves and to the heart of God is to love each other in our disagreement, to be authentic to ourselves yet authentic to the community of faith of which we are a part.

There's a wonderful hymn with words such as these: "Whether our tomorrows be filled with good or ill, we'll triumph through our sorrows and rise to bless you still."[17] Our tomorrows are in jeopardy. However, to listen to the heart of God is a dangerous game, because we can never really know the realities of the Divine. Even so, we are called to follow the voice of the Divine. We are called to listen as best we can. Listening requires us to forsake our certainty and begin to love everyone, even those who disagree with us. The Spirit of God is moving in our world, and I would hate it if the church missed that movement. Within our time and our place, let us face these issues with the same dignity and grace that called Christ to come to this earth. There is difficulty in loving, but it is a good start when we want to listen to God.

---

17. Michael Perry, "O God beyond All Praising" (Carol Stream, IL: Hope Publishing Co., 1981).

EQUALITY IS PART OF GOD'S DREAM FOR THE WORLD

SUMMER 2013

Over the past couple of weeks, we have all grappled with the sensitive subjects of race, equality, and justice in light of the George Zimmerman verdict that has captivated our nation.[18] I have been reading your thoughts and feelings through your letters to the editor, through various comments, and through social media. Many people have opined on the merits of our justice system, the status of racial equality in our nation, and the realities of living in community with one another.

So where does faith come into this situation? How do we react faithfully and find the hope of God in the midst of such a climate of polarization?

First, let's establish that it isn't faithful for us to be "colorblind" as some people have suggested. To ignore our cultural, racial, and ethnic identities is to ignore a beautiful gift our creator has given us all. We all have to come to a realization of how we enter into the dance of life. For instance, I am a white man and I have to acknowledge that.

However, I can't suggest that I know what it's like to be a woman, a person of color, or anyone with a background other than my own. I come to the conversation with my own identity, and we must all strive to be like that.

Second, while our race is a gift from God, the gifts that God has given us have not been treated equally in our collective history. We cannot be

---

18. On July 13, 2013, a Florida jury found George Zimmerman not guilty of second-degree murder in the February 2012 shooting death of seventeen-year-old Trayvon Martin.

faithful by simply saying that since we were not around during the Civil War or, for some of us, during the racial tensions of Jim Crow South, we are somehow not responsible for the implications of the past. Since the dawn of humankind, God has been about reconciling; God has brought the people who often fell wayward back to God's self. But God is also clear that we are on this journey together. We are a chain that stretches throughout time, and we cannot ignore the past simply because we weren't there.

How can we be faithful? How can we address the tensions of our time and find grace in the midst of it? The reality is that we must recognize our differences and celebrate them! We must work with organizations in our community such as Habitat for Humanity, Iredell Christian Ministries, and others that reach across socioeconomic, racial, ethnic, and political bounds to give and receive the love of Christ. For it is Christ who reminds us that our neighbor isn't always the people who look like us or sound like us. It could be a boy on his way to get Skittles, it might be a man who is on trial, or maybe it's someone so foreign from us that we can't comprehend God loving them.

God is all about making the circle wider. God is all about grace and reconciliation and redemption. So when we are faithful to the conversations about race and the dignity of human life, we are faithful to a God who loves all of us as his own.

PUBLIC THEOLOGY AND TAYLOR SWIFT

SEPTEMBER 27, 2017

Author's note: This article appeared in the Huffington Post as well as the Record & Landmark.

It's confession time: I'm a huge Taylor Swift fan. I'm starting to identify with her more now that I've been thrust into the realm of public theology. People often bemoan Swift as someone who complains about media attention or how others treat her. As my story grew about my resignation from my parish and the ensuing conversations on platforms like NPR and *The View*, I've found that people are, in fact, incredibly mean in the face of media attention.

Twitter trolls can be vicious and scrutiny is real, but the cost of not engaging in public theology is far greater than one might think. I've had friends and mentors who have been concerned for my health and safety tell me to back off the gas pedal a bit and find greener pastures elsewhere. But perhaps this moment of speaking truth to power is no time for falling back.

As I write these words, I'm just on the other side of my twenty-fifth birthday. Had you told my wife and me when we were married a mere three months ago that we would be on this road heading to God knows where, I would have laughed and sat back down in my pastoral chair. You may be wondering what this has to do with you. We must always be ready to engage the world and the church in new and different ways.

In a sense, we must *shake it off* (yes, I went there) and do the hard work of engaging in beloved community. We must seek the resolution of these issues that are close at hand and be public theologians. We desperately need to add names to the dwindling list of public theologians in our world, and we desperately need some of those names to be millennials. The reality is that we have to consider how we can engage church differently for the sake of our future.

I'm not one to suggest that we abandon the institution, but we must reignite the passion that led to white pastors marching in the civil rights movement alongside their brothers and sisters of color. This critical engagement with the world is precisely what the world needs to see right now. We need not worry about empty pews if our hearts are apathetic to the world we see, because the pews should be empty if that is the case. But I refuse to believe that. I refuse to believe that the white church can't engage in anti-racism conversations or that the wider church can't engage our LGBTQ friends with dignity and acceptance.

What I'm getting at is this: we need public theology. The other forces of this world (including Evangelical and Fundamentalist Christians) are engaging in public theology. What makes progressive Christians think we get a free pass? Now is the time to engage the world with a different and fresh way of doing progressive Christianity. It is in that hope that we see in God we have more future than past. God has given us possibility, hope, and courage, and that is better than any pain our past holds. We could shake the foundations of this nation and world for the sake of our children and our children's children. I've been thankful that trolls are just trolls, but they've taught me that speaking up costs something, and I really am indebted to my favorite pop star Taylor Swift for the inspiration to speak up in the form of public theology and say, "Look what you made me do."

TO STEPHANIE, ON THE OCCASION OF OUR WEDDING

MAY 25, 2017

I rarely try to use this space and column as a personal platform, but as the week progressed I found myself focusing on one thing and one thing only: I marry the love of my life on Saturday at Broad Street United Methodist Church, the place where I was baptized in 1992 and the place where my brother and father who will serve as my best men were baptized.

I wanted to reflect on what my soon-to-be wife has taught me about God these past four years of knowing her. In so doing, I hope you can see in your spouse or partner what God is doing in your life.

1. Just as Abram and Sarai said "yes" to God's unfolding future, Stephanie has taught me to throw off the bow lines and sail away from safe harbor (to borrow from Mark Twain).

2. Just as Joseph forgave his brothers, Stephanie has shown me forgiveness and love that I didn't always deserve.

3. Just as Moses parted the Red Sea, Stephanie, under the influence of Divine power, has made a way where there was no way.

4. Just as Elijah spoke a fitting word for a tumultuous time, Stephanie has seen me at my worst and always known what to say.

5. Just as Ruth turned toward Naomi and went with her into unknown territory, Stephanie has done likewise.

6. Just as Mordecai said to Esther, "for such a time as this," Stephanie has always encouraged me to reach for my dreams and hopes, like going to Duke Divinity School or applying for jobs.

7. Just as the prophets spoke of God's design and plan, Stephanie always has me sticking to our plan.

8. Just as James said faith without works is dead, Stephanie is always putting her faith to work.

9. Just as the Blessed Virgin Mary and Jesus went to the wedding at Cana in Galilee, we will celebrate on Saturday and call this union blessed.

I say these things not to put Stephanie on a pedestal; she wouldn't want that. What I am saying is that we have been to hell and back, and Stephanie hasn't shrunk back. Just as I see Stephanie in the beauty of the biblical narrative, I challenge you to see yourself, your family, your spouse there too. For in Scripture we see the full range of human experience. We see that God is with us and God is for us.

Stephanie, I can't bring you fortune, and I can't bring you fame, but I will always attempt to love you as Christ loves the church (Eph 5:25), and if you know how much I love the church, you will realize that is an undying and faithful love. You are a beautiful soul who has challenged and shaped me by the grace of God, and I am so lucky to be your husband on Saturday.

"For all that has been, thanks. For all that will be, yes!"[19]

With all my love,
Rob

---

19. Dag Hammarskjöld, January 1953.

FAITH AND THE CONFEDERATE FLAG

JUNE 23, 2016

My family bloodline is bound up in a dark part of American history. With a name like Robert Lee, the question I undoubtedly receive most about my name is, "Are you related to him?" And the answer is yes. Yes, I am. I am a descendant of the Lees of Virginia, and whenever I visit the Arlington House at Arlington National Cemetery, I see where my family lived and played and, yes, owned people. I see where Robert Edward Lee, my ancestor, spent probably sleepless nights deciding what to do about the problem our nation faced.

Naturally, when I was younger, I wanted to know everything about where I came from. I wanted to know all about this general in the Army of Northern Virginia, but as I grew in knowledge and stature, I found myself incredibly conflicted and riddled with guilt. I had a small Confederate flag, given to me by a friend to remind me of my heritage. I don't know where that flag is anymore, and frankly that's for the best.

You see, white Christians cannot sit by while our Black brothers and sisters are echoing the words of Psalm 13: "How long, O Lord?" We cannot be the white moderates that Dr. King spoke of when he said, "Shallow understanding from people of goodwill is more frustrating than absolute misunderstanding from people of ill will. Lukewarm acceptance is much more bewildering than outright rejection."[20]

As a Lee, I am sorry for my history. I am sorry that people were viewed and treated as property by my family. But more important, I'm sorry that most of us have been shallow in our understanding. It's time for the people

---

20. Martin Luther King Jr., "Letter from Birmingham Jail," April 16, 1963 (africa.upenn.edu/Articles_Gen/Letter_Birmingham.html).

of the South to take the flag down, because for all of us, it should be a faith issue.

The Jesus we follow beckons us to a greater understanding of human dignity. For in human dignity we see the incarnation of God. God loved us to the point that he came to first-century Palestine in a time of misunderstanding much like our own. He challenged the comfortable and overturned tables that needed to be overturned. Now is our opportunity to challenge and overturn what is wrong in the eyes of sensibility and human dignity.

Please hear me when I say we can't ignore our heritage and where we come from. It is impossible. I cannot escape my history of being a descendant of someone who fought to divide this nation. But I can have a response to my history that is healthy and beautiful. I'm reminded of what one of my favorite preachers once said: "If it can't be happy, make it beautiful." Nothing we can do about the history of racism and prejudice in the South can be happy. It is a sad reality we are called to face. But our response, how we live into the future, can be really beautiful and something to celebrate; it can be more freeing for everyone than we could ever possibly imagine.

God is somewhere in the midst of this, working to make things beautiful. But God cannot simply rid us of our history. We must work to make true the love of Jesus. We must work to make true the words of the saints who fought and are fighting for civil rights. So, as a Lee whose history is dark, and as a Lee with whatever privilege that provides me, it's time to take down the flag and begin the long road to reconciliation that God offers us.

HOLIDAYS AND HOLY DAYS

The task of liturgy is to order the life of the holy community following the text of Holy Scripture. It consists of two movements. First it gets us into the sanctuary, the place of adoration and attention, listening and receiving and believing before God. There is a lot involved, all the parts of our lives ordered to all aspects of the revelation of God in Jesus. Then it gets us out of the sanctuary into the world into places of obeying and loving, ordering our lives as living sacrifices in the world to the glory of God. There is a lot involved, all the parts of our lives out on the street participating in the work of salvation.

—Eugene H. Peterson (from Eat this Book: A Conversation in the Art of Spiritual Reading)

A considerable amount of my time with the *Statesville Record & Landmark* was spent working with the secular calendar to make it holy—and remind the holy that it need not be secularized. But then I realized that there is beauty in both, and both should be celebrated as best they can. The secular and sacred aren't held in tension but in hope-filled unity. Here are just a few of the articles that transcend the calendar.

THE LIGHTS OF HANUKKAH BURN BRIGHT, RENEW FAITH

DECEMBER 19, 2014

Every year around this time, I love to send Hanukkah cards to my Jewish friends who celebrate and mark Hanukkah as I prepare to celebrate Christmas. This Festival of Lights is an eight-day Jewish holiday commemorating the dedication of the second temple in Jerusalem at the time of the Revolt of the Maccabees during the second century.

The story goes that pure olive oil with the seal of the high priest was required for the menorah in the temple, which was supposed to burn throughout every night. It is said that there was only enough oil to burn for one day, but it burned for eight days straight. By the time the eight days were over, there was more oil blessed and consecrated for use in the temple.

What does this mean for our faith? Both Jews and Christians can appreciate miracles—I am confident in that. Our shared heritage makes this an important moment for both faiths. Even though Christians can often ignore it, it is important to mark this holy time with our Jewish brothers and sisters.

The lights of Hanukkah this year remind us of the hope, love, and peace that we so desperately need in this world. The lights of Hanukkah remind us that darkness cannot overcome light and that the God of our forefathers and foremothers is still present to this day, working to banish darkness in whatever form it presents itself.

Dear Jewish friends, know that I have been praying for you these cold winter nights as you light candles. It is my prayer that your candles may burn brighter each night and that you find consolation that darkness is no match for God.

Dear Christian friends, I ask you to join me in prayer for our Jewish friends. I offer a prayer below that you might be able to say for them. It is my hope that you will join me in this time of celebration, for this is an important moment for many across our land. May the lights of Hanukkah enliven all our hearts as we commemorate God's miraculous presence. Thanks be to God!

A Prayer for Hanukkah: *God of us all, bless all those who celebrate Hanukkah. May the lights they light shine forth into the world and be a reminder of God's presence. Amen.*

SHARING FAITH: BE MORE LIKE HOWARD ADLER

DECEMBER 22, 2016

I didn't know Howard Adler well; in fact, I only met him once years ago when my church went over to visit Congregation Emmanuel Temple just across the way. Mr. Adler opened the synagogue to our church group and patiently explained the beauty of his faith to curious, albeit skeptical youngsters.

I was helping my mom chaperone that trip, and I'll never forget his willingness to tell the sacred story of his life and journey, from escaping Nazi Germany to living a life full of service. No moment was off limits for questions by our youth group from Broad Street. You may be wondering why I'm telling you this. Mr. Adler died this week at the age of ninety-nine—a life well lived, if you ask me or anyone else in this town.

As we light the lights of Hanukkah and gather close around the table of the Eucharist this Christmas and Hanukkah weekend, may we all strive to be a little more like Mr. Adler. We may not have incredible stories of heroism in the face of genocide, but we all have our stories, and that is what makes us who we are. We are people who live together in community, and that story is worth sharing. Every time I write a column for you all, I try to think about a takeaway message I want you to carry with you. On this most holy of weekends, this is what I hope you will espouse: you are full of sacred worth by a loving and living God, a God who has bent down since Abraham and Sarah and has shown us the way. May our faith give light to the hope that God is still working, still mending, still re-creating, and, yes, still redeeming this troubled globe.

The next time someone asks you about the sacred story of your faith, may you be like Mr. Adler and never be afraid to share your faith with the world. May our story reflect the sacredness of who we are and who our God is. Though Adler's light may be gone from this world, it's our opportunity to carry on the legacy of goodness, kindness, and peace. May we be bold in our proclamation of the sacred story of our faith. May we be brave in the face of persecution and wrongdoing, and may we hold fast to all that we know is good in this world. Therein lies our hope. May the lights of Christmas and Hanukkah shine brightly in our hearts this week. That's all we could ever hope for.

May your holidays be bright. Amen.

O LITTLE TOWN OF STATESVILLE

DECEMBER 21, 2017

You all know how the hymn goes: "O little town of Bethlehem, how still we see thee lie; above thy deep and dreamless sleep the silent stars go by. Yet in thy dark street shineth the everlasting light; the hopes and fears of all the years are met in thee tonight."

For some reason, I can't get the comparison of the little town of Bethlehem and the little town of Statesville out of my head. You see, my wife Stephanie and I have come down off the mountain and moved back into the neighborhood. This week, we closed on a house in Statesville. And there's something about Statesville with its historic charm that reminds me of a land in Judea far away and a long time ago nestled at the edge of an empire.

You see, as Steph and I are unpacking boxes, I'm also visiting with a family whose father is dying. I'm catching up with a friend at Wine Maestro whom I hadn't seen in over five years. Amid the hustle and hype of the holidays, I see that Christ came for each and every one of us.

Christ came for the man who's in hospice care. Christ came for the friend who may not fully get the whole "faith thing." Christ came for me, who always tries to be everything for everybody. Christ came for you whoever you are and wherever you find yourself this Christmas.

I don't have all the answers, but the work of Christmas is done in moments like these. The world may be crashing in around us, but by God, Christ came to an empire that was breathing with anticipation for the next stage.

Be ready for Christ this Christmas. The Blessed Virgin Mary took the blessing of saying yes to God and allowed the world to be blessed through her. How will you return in kind? How will you say yes to God so that the hope of the world is found amid the busyness of this season? It is a holy moment; it is a silent night. Make ready, for Christ is here.

WHAT MATTERS MOST IN LIFE ISN'T TANGIBLE

DECEMBER 13, 2013

If you're anywhere near or have any contact with a college student this week, they will tell you this is one of the hardest times of the year for us. We'll take the final exams that combine a semester's worth of material into one, final, all-encompassing test to show our knowledge and skills gained from the course we have just completed. It's daunting to say the least.

As I prepared for finals, I couldn't help but think that these experiences we go through in life are microcosms of our faith. We all experience that final exam one day. We all have to give an account as to what mattered most to us in life. The question is, how are you preparing to give an answer?

Advent, this season of expectancy, is a time to prepare for such a question. Advent not only expects the Christ child to come in the manger at Christmas but also expects the ultimate return of Jesus in triumphant victory over evil. So this season we are playing two different games with similar rules: we expect the past to open up wonder in us once again, and we expect the fruition of God's promise in the future.

This week, I am reminded of the human effort of finals. But I am also reminded of what was once said by philosopher and theologian Eberhard Arnold:

> Christmas did not come after a great horde of people had completed something good, or because of the successful result of any human effort. No, it came as a miracle, as the child that comes when his time is fulfilled. This is how the first Christmas came; in this way

it always comes anew, both to us as individuals and to the whole world.[21]

Challenge yourself—what really matters right now? Is it finals, work, getting the best gift? Or do you find your hope and true meaning in the beauty of a candlelight Christmas, when the world breathes a sigh of relief because Christ has burst onto the scene? Perhaps you're like me, hurrying about with finals and assignments, trying to get it all done before the deadline. But then I think of the coming Christ child who reminds us that being busy is not the answer to our existence. The answer is found in a manger.

It is in those moments that I realize I will have to give an account not of my GPA or the job I land after college but of how I found the Christ child in my own life. What matters isn't the tangible success of this world but the inward humbling of a beautiful grace. May we be so bold as to proclaim this from the tops of mountains and in the lowest valleys. Make way for our coming King. Are you excited for Christmas yet?

---

21. "When the Time Was Fulfilled" in *When the Time Was Fulfilled* (Walden, NY: Plough Publishing House, 2007), 10.

THE CHRISTMAS SPIRIT, ALIVE IN EACH OF US

DECEMBER 20, 2013

John Denver and the Muppets: A Christmas Together is definitely my favorite Christmas album. I have it on my iPhone, CD, and vinyl.

One of my favorite songs on the album is titled "The Peace Carol." Part of the song goes like this:

> The garment of life, be it tattered and torn,
> the cloak of the soldier is withered and worn.
> But what child is this that was poverty-born, the peace of Christmas Day.
> . . .
> The hope that has slumbered for 2000 years,
> the promise that silenced 1000 fears.
> A faith that can hobble an ocean of tears, the peace of Christmas Day.

Friends, we come to this fruition of our Advent season with 2000 years of expectation. We have yearned for the incarnation to happen. We have lit candles, we have sung carols at the top of our lungs, but now it's here. Christmas is just around the corner, and we have much to celebrate.

However, I want to remind all of you of something very important. Not everyone will have a merry and happy Christmas this year. There is pain, there is heartache, and there is a tattered and torn reality for many who suffer this time of year. The holidays are not always joyful, and we as a people must be mindful of that.

So whatever your situation is this year, be it merry or not, remember that the incarnation happened and happens again this year for you. You are the reason the God of all creation became human; you are the love that God has been waiting for. You are the reason for the Advent of our God.

I am reminded that Teresa of Avila said, "Christ has no body but yours, no hands or feet on earth but yours." This year, you have the potential to bring about Christmas to someone who is hurting and in pain. You have the potential to play an active role in the incarnation.

These past few weeks, I have opined on the importance of preparing, expecting, and waiting. Now, as we reach the fruition of everything we hold dear, as the hopes and fears of all the years are met in Christ our Lord, may you have a blessed holiday, and may you be a part of the life-changing grace that God offers to each of us. When Christmas comes, find the beauty of the season and the hope of the incarnation. Merry Christmas, dear friends. Merry Christmas.

THE HUSTLE AND BUSTLE OF CHRISTMAS

DECEMBER 2012

The other day I was busy shopping around stores here in Boone. I walked into Walmart in my usual rush to get things done. It's not my favorite store in the world, so I try to make it in and out as quickly as possible, seeing the fewest people I know. I guess I'm just one of those people who is on a mission and doesn't want distractions.

That being said, a gentleman with developmental disabilities stopped me. I had no idea what he wanted or what he needed, but I was sure it wasn't as important as me getting my errands done.

He simply and directly changed my perspective on this season. He looked at me and said, "I just think you need to have someone wish you a merry Christmas. Have a good day!" I was humbled beyond any explanation that I could ever give. God has a way of doing that with situations like that, don't you agree?

In this season of preparation for Christmas, it's easy to get lost in the hustle and bustle of this time. We forget the real reason we're even preparing for that glorious day. We forget that in these moments we are on the verge of hopes and fears of all the years being met in an incarnate God. Keep the faith that this is a time when we are on the verge of a dream.

On the verge of a dream—I think we've all been there in our lives. We've all been on the cusp of something great, and we can't wait to see what it is. But if anything, this season has taught me that patience and waiting are part of faith. We cannot have faith without a healthy dose of patience and waiting for the fruition of what God has in store.

This week, take time to breathe. All the errands will be run; all the decorations will be put up. All will be well. We are on the verge of something great, and it's our duty to bask in the glory of what is to come. People, get ready—Jesus is coming![22]

I echo the words of my friend from Walmart: "I just think you need to have someone wish you a merry Christmas. Have a good day!"

---

22. Brian Ray, "People, Get Ready . . . Jesus Is Comin'," recorded by Crystal Lewis, *Beauty for Ashes*.

WE NEED THE HOPE OF CHRISTMAS NOW

NOVEMBER 18, 2018

I put my Christmas tree up November 2. Now, you may think I'm crazy, but I'm starting to think residents of this fine town should consider putting our Christmas trees up early this year.

Simply and directly, our world is not what it should be. And the Advent and Christmas season offer the expectancy of what should be.

Our world seems hell-bent on self-destruction, but God who became incarnate in Christ offers us a different way, a better way. A way that is pregnant with anticipation for the love that we might share with one another.

I think one of my greatest regrets is that for the first twenty-six years of my life, I was a liturgical Scrooge who wanted nothing to do with carols and tinsel until sundown on Christmas Eve, when the church marks the beginning of Christmas. I know I will be in trouble for saying this, but perhaps the church needs to reconsider.

Since before the dawn of time, humanity has yearned for a better way of doing things. As we evolved into the twenty-first century, we have seen the proliferation of technology, of culture, of life itself. But we have also experienced tragedy and war and pain, and we remain divided and sad. But the hope of Christmas, at least for me, is learning to believe in the basics of faith again: that God in God's goodness loved the created order enough to engage with it.

You may be thinking we're too far gone for that, but I implore you to consider the hope of the season of Advent and Christmas and maybe, just maybe, engage in the incarnation a little early this year.

So go ahead. Put your tree up, decorate it, spend time with your family, and enjoy the season, because we need a little Christmas right this very minute. We need the hope of Christ coming to earth both then and there and here and now.

Isn't it a magnificent story? The most amazing part about it for me is that it can happen again. Every time we love the other, every time we welcome the stranger or visit someone in prison, we are doing so to the Christ we worship.

Perhaps this year you can buck tradition and put up your tree early.

Perhaps this year you could give in and volunteer at the soup kitchen.

Perhaps this is the year you call your parents and try to make amends.

Perhaps this year you can get help for your mental illness.

Whatever it is, let this be the year for change and for hope. We need those two things now more than ever.

IF NOT NOW, WHEN?

JANUARY, 12, 2017

I hope you'll consider joining us at the annual Martin Luther King Jr. festivities in Statesville this weekend. From a day of service to a prayer breakfast, Statesville will commemorate the life of the Rev. Dr. Martin Luther King Jr. and the countless sung and unsung heroes of the civil rights movement. This year's theme is "If not now, when?"

This past fall, I had the honor of touring the new Smithsonian National Museum of African American History. And that museum reminded me of something we all need to hear: throughout this nation's history, despite what seemed like insurmountable odds, people of color have maintained a sense of resiliency and tenacity the likes of which this world has never seen. In countless instances of institutional and systemic racism, from the slave trade to reconstruction to Jim Crow to Ferguson, we have witnessed the ability of African Americans to speak truth to power, to dream of a better tomorrow, and to claim the God they know as Lord.

It's a daunting task for me to have been invited to speak at the civic center on Monday for the prayer breakfast. Growing up as a white kid in the South presented me with enormous privilege, and it has caused me to wonder at what point will we bend the arc of the universe toward justice, equity, and mutual respect.[23]

---

23. "The arc of the moral universe is long, but it bends toward justice" is MLK's famous paraphrase of nineteenth-century Unitarian minister, reformer, and abolitionist Theodore Parker, who wrote, "I do not pretend to understand the moral universe; the arc is a long one, my eye reaches but little ways; I cannot calculate the curve and complete the figure by the experience of sight; I can divine it by conscience. And from what I see I am sure it bends towards justice" ("Theodore Parker and the 'Moral Universe,'" *All Things Considered*, NPR.com, September 2, 2010 [npr.org/templates/story/story.php?storyId=129609461]).

You see, that's what God has in mind for us. God created us in God's image, and God saw that we were good. God saw that the whole of creation was good, and we must honor that. If not now, when? If not now, when will we acknowledge the dignity and respect deserved by every human person?

We live in what seem like insurmountable odds as a nation due to racism and phobias, but the God we serve beckons us toward wholeness. All lives cannot matter until we push for the dignity of black lives. God is deeply connected with the movement of justice, and we must be as well. Be sure to check out the events this weekend and on Martin Luther King Day. They're worth your time, because if not now, when?

WEDDING PLANNING TEACHES ABOUT LENT

MARCH 3, 2016

Stephanie and I are a power couple. We like to have things planned and laid out and ready to go for any possible scenario. So when we announced our engagement to the world last Thursday, one of the first questions we received was, "When and where?" Stephanie and I both sensed a need to begin planning, so after basking in our engagement for a while we proceeded to start talking about possibilities.

They say if a couple can successfully plan a wedding together, there is nothing they can't do. All of you who have traversed this terrain before know what Stephanie and I are going through, carefully crafting a master plan for our special day. Planning a budget and reserving venues, clergy, musicians, and the like is no small task, and there's a lot going on in our lives with me at the divinity school and Stephanie's impending graduation. I articulated how much was on our plate to my Nana, and she said something profound: "All this planning and something will most certainly go wrong, but don't worry. It's not about the planning; it's about the person you're with."

Fade scene to Jesus walking up the hill to Jerusalem, preparing for the triumphant entry on Palm Sunday and the week that is to come and that we will mark in just a few short weeks. You see, in the church year, we are smack-dab in the middle of Lent. I'm sure the disciples weren't exactly sure what to think when Jesus changed the Passover meal into the first Holy Communion. I'm sure they had great Passover plans, but I like to use my scriptural imagination to picture Jesus telling them something similar to what my Nana said.

That's the danger of following Jesus. He didn't fit the mold of Messiah when he got down and washed feet or when he changed wine and bread into his body and blood. Jesus changes our neatly formed plans into something different, something holy. The disciples had no idea what lay before them, but the Easter that came after that trumped all their planning and their plans. They were made whole and holy.

While I know the dangers of comparing planning a wedding to Holy Week, I think you all know what I'm getting at. We all have these neatly formed ideas of what should be done and how it should be done and why it should be done. But when Good Friday happens, we, like Jesus' chosen few, scatter and run. We are afraid to continue for fear of more wrong happening, but that's not a way to live.

Stephanie and I are so excited for our special day. We've been told that it won't go off perfectly, but I'm starting to think that's what will make our day holy and wholly perfect. So the next time you have to plan a wedding or attend a wedding, think of all the planning that went into it and the beauty of the day, but also remember that God is bigger than our plans and interjects grace upon grace into those moments we will come to cherish.

AN INVITATION TO SLOW DOWN DURING LENT

MARCH 2, 2017

As I write this, I have the flu. I was diagnosed with it Monday and have been forced to slow down for a few days as my body begins to rest and recover. I know the flu is a terrible thing, but this time around, I'm considering it a blessing in disguise for me. This is because it has forced me to slow down as Lent begins this week.

We spend our lives trying to hurry from one thing to the next, so as I was forced to stay around the house and take a second to breathe and recover, I was reminded of the importance of taking stock of things, of slowing down, and of smelling the flowers.

I can't tell you the last time I've had to stick around the house and simply be present and rest. I know we all don't have that luxury, but let me offer you three ideas for a holy and slow Lent.

1. If you must be in a hurry, make haste to love and not to judge. Make haste to hope and not to despair; make haste to show grace and not to condemn; make haste to show joy and not sadness.

2. If you can slow down, enjoy every moment of it. Turn the phone and social media off, and bask in the glory of being disconnected. We spend our lives tethered to people and technology; I'm just as guilty. Jesus walked a lonely road, and perhaps a holy loneliness can give clarity and reassurance.

3. Finally, give up something like you usually do for Lent, but this year, give up more than chocolate or soda. Perhaps give up the preconceived notion you have of someone at work or school, or give up the clique and reach out to someone new. This enables you to truly observe a holy and Christ-like Lenten season.

These are just a few ideas for Lent. What are yours? How are you observing Lent this year? These forty days of penitence and Passiontide are the culmination of the ministry of Jesus, a ministry built on deep love and commitment to the heart of God. May we be brave in our love and our deep commitment to that heart as well.

Blessings to you this Lent, and may it prepare you for the Easter we are already looking forward to so diligently.

LENT IS A TIME TO ADJUST

FEBRUARY 20, 2015

The church year has brought us to Lent, the time of penitence and self-reflection before Good Friday and Easter Sunday. I once heard it said that you can't have Easter without Lent; how could you know the joy of the mountaintop without the realities of the valley?

I tried to think of this in a few practical ways. I have a member at the church I serve who is a chiropractor. A few weekends ago, I spent eight hours in a car driving our youth on a trip. When I returned, I needed someone to look at my back and neck, which were incredibly sore. I had to have my back adjusted. Our lives are like that. We go throughout life thinking we're invincible and full of everything we need until it comes time for us to need an adjustment—that's what Lent is for.

Lent is a time when people give up bad habits, work on spiritual disciplines, and remind ourselves of the love of God present in our lives. We work hard to remind ourselves that Lent is as much a part of our lives as Easter is.

So this week as you ponder your own life and the Lenten journey you are on, what needs to be adjusted? What needs to be changed, deleted, or added to your life to make your walk with God a more fruitful one? As you think through this, hopefully you'll find that adjusting your life can change its trajectory. You can change things about your life, and, through God's help, all things can be made new.

Perhaps look at it this way: Occasionally I find myself adding coolant to my car because my car has some coolant issues. I have to add the coolant to keep the car running. We, too, must keep adding to our faith and adjusting our faith to keep faith fresh, new, and alive. What are you doing to add to your faith? How are you self-examining yourself this Lent? How are you finding yourself enveloped in the grace of your Creator in spite of the darkness of this world?

Keep the faith that God is at work this Lenten season. Remember that it's important that your spiritual life is fresh and new. Ultimately, spirituality is fluid, and we must be observant of what we are doing in our lives. Be prepared, though, because God might show up and turn your faith upside down, and that's a wonderful thing.

MARK LENT FAITHFULLY

FEBRUARY 20, 2015

This past Wednesday was the start of Lent, Ash Wednesday. Every year, the church marks the forty days before Easter in an effort to remind us of our mortality and our need for repentance. This is countercultural to our twenty-first-century sensibilities. Mortality is something we're afraid to talk about because it is scary, but that is precisely where Jesus is leading us this Lenten season.

Each Ash Wednesday, we mark our brow with the sign of the Lamb who was slain as a reminder that from dust we were created and to dust we shall return. It is in that mindset that we mark the passage of these forty days. We are reminded of our need for grace; we are reminded of our need for resurrection. But resurrection during Lent seems far off and distant. That's because our lives are not always as close to resurrection as they ought to be.

This Lent, I challenge you to take on a spiritual practice or give something up in the hopes of catching a glimpse of resurrection. These glimpses of new life are what get us through the dark times, the times when life doesn't make sense or evil seems to be winning.

Keep the faith that God is at work. Keep the faith that just because you have ashes on your forehead, that is not your eternal destiny. Actually, it's quite the contrary. Our lives are wrapped up in eternal hope. Thanks be to God for Lent. May you be abundantly blessed this season and on your journey.

GOD IS PRESENT IN THE SILENCE

SUMMER 2014

Is it just me, or have there been a number of Bible-based movies and television series in the past few months?

This past week, I decided to grab some popcorn and go see *Noah*, starring Russell Crowe, Emma Watson, Sir Anthony Hopkins, and others. This movie chronicles the adventures of one of the Bible's most well-known stories in a very different light. If you are looking for biblical correctness, you won't find it in this movie. But that's not the point I want to talk about today. I want to talk about the beauty of the silence of God.

In the movie, Noah is strangely perplexed, as God is strangely silent at important points in which it would be nice for God to show up. That got me thinking about our lives of faith. During this season of Lent, we talk a lot about darkness, a lot about silence, and a lot about despair.

We don't like to think of God as silent; we don't like to think there are points in our lives when we cry out to God and only hear silence. But perhaps in the silence God is speaking and we just can't hear it. This reminds me of a newer hymn titled "Holy Darkness" with lyrics like this: "Holy darkness, blessed night, heaven's answer hidden from our sight. As we wait for you, O God of silence, we embrace your holy night."[24]

As hard as silence is, God can be found when we least expect God. In the breeze, in the sunrise, in the quietness before a church service, God is present and loving us through our darkness.

The hymn goes on, "As the watchman waits for morning, and the bride awaits her groom, so we wait to hear footsteps as we rest beneath your moon." Even at night, God gave us the moon for the hope of the morning;

---

24. Dan Schutte, "Holy Darkness" (Portland, OR: OCP, 1988).

even in our death, we have the hope of resurrection—all of this in the knowledge that we are afraid of silence. Isn't it marvelous that God comes to us in our fears and meets us there?

This week, be sure to embrace the silence, because God can be found there. Be sure to find the beauty of the silent and loving God, because even in the silence God has the power to speak. Thanks be to God.

LENT AND FINDING FAITH IN *FAMILY GUY*

MAY 31, 2014

There's an episode of *Family Guy* where Mort Goldman comes over to Peter Griffin's house and asks to borrow a crucifix. Mort says, "Preferably one without the little fellow on it."

Doesn't that sound like the Lenten season? Lent is dark and messy. We don't like the image of Jesus on the cross because, ultimately, it's not a Jesus who is easy to imagine with our holy imagination. Though *Family Guy* is a comedy, it has a point: we like the cross without Jesus.

Western society has done an incredible job of taking the cross and making it into something it's not.

Whether we attribute it to taboos, culture, or a lack of education, we view the cross very differently than the earliest Christians viewed it. As Mary Button says, "We can only begin to understand the meaning of the crucifixion when we take away our polished and shiny crosses and try to locate the cross in our own time, and in our own landscape."

The meaning of the crucifixion is this: we threw the worst we could at Jesus, capital punishment in the vilest form, and God brought about Easter morning. Throughout all of human history, we've done a pretty good job of silencing the hope, justice, and grace extended to us by our Creator. The cross stands as a reminder that there is nothing that can't be accomplished by the God of the resurrection.

So this Lenten season, let's be living reminders that the cross does not have the final say, that atonement is accomplished by the glory of the incarnation and the resurrection. The cross tried to get in the way, but God worked through the reality of the cross to bring about life. From death came life; from finite time eternity was born. Remember that the cross is more than a necklace, a pretty ornate object that we bow to in church, or a means of propaganda. The cross is a reminder of the darkness of human ignorance, but, more important, it's a reminder of the glory of God's victory over death.

Perhaps now you can let Jesus be on the cross. You can let him stay in the grips of death because it shows that God experienced all that we could possibly experience. However, let's not leave him there. Let our lives be living reminders that the resurrection happens after the cross.

When I was younger, my brother and I had Lenten figurines that represented the cross and the tomb. Jesus was fixed to the cross, but to my little brother's dismay, you couldn't get Jesus off the cross for Easter. My little brother said he wanted a "walking around Jesus," so my parents searched until they found a figure that matched our set that had Jesus walking around.

Ultimately, the point of Lent is this: it is transient. The cross is transient, and the hope of the coming Easter is that Jesus will walk around once more. May we be prepared for all that's in store. Thanks be to God.

MAKE THE MOST OF HOLY WEEK

MARCH 27, 2015

I love worship. If I could spend the rest of my academic career studying worship, I would. Of course, at divinity school you have to study other things, but I'm most excited for my worship classes.

That being said, I think there is also something to be said about participating in worship, especially during this season.

Next week the Christian tradition is marked as Holy Week as we approach Good Friday and Easter Sunday. I'd encourage you to mark Holy Week faithfully; don't just jump to Easter! It's easy for us to skip Holy Week because we don't like to talk about the dark things of our lives, but this week is precisely where Jesus calls us to go.

You see, in the darkness of Holy Week we realize the importance of Easter. I would encourage you to attend a Holy Week service. There are plenty of opportunities: Palm Sunday, Maundy Thursday, Good Friday, Easter Vigil, and, of course, let it all culminate with Easter Sunday. Allow God to work through the services that you are a part of because God gave everything this week that we mark.

So linger a while in Holy Week just like I challenged you all to linger in Lent. From the loud shouts of Hosanna on Palm Sunday to the "It is finished" on Good Friday, we see the love and grace mingled with blood and tears in the hope of the resurrection to come. It is through these moments of Holy Week that we come close to the heart of God.

Don't let the darkness of the season keep your eyes from the promise of Easter. Even in Lent there are traces of resurrection, and that can be true in our worship experiences. I encourage you to look at the calendar of your church and find a time where you can worship the God who became like us. But take heart: Jesus is the Word become flesh, and you can't keep the

Word dead for long. Thanks be to God that we have Holy Week and the promise of Easter.

PASSOVER IS A TIME TO TALK ABOUT FREEDOM

APRIL 18, 2014

Before I say anything today, I want to acknowledge that I have not walked the path of the Hebrew faith and have not lived with the violence and oppression of our ancestors in faith. However, I hope that we can come to understand and more deeply appreciate the tradition of the Passover, regardless of our faith tradition.

Jewish people across our world this week are celebrating their ancestors' exodus from Egypt. They seek more fully to commemorate the love God has for God's chosen people and to remember that even under Pharaoh's hand, God could send a person like Moses to lead God's people to freedom.

Passover began Monday, and I want us to all take a lesson from what God did in the lives of the Israelites. Today, God is working to bring us all to freedom in the face of whatever form oppression takes. There is a healing balm in the hope that we are bound for the promised land, and the beauty of the exodus story is that God did not forget God's people.

The grace of everything we hold dear is bound up in our freedom and our future. God knows that, and God continually works to bring us to freedom through the seas of our existence. God binds up whatever Pharaoh we are facing and reminds us of the preciousness of our existence.

This week, pray for the people of the Jewish faith celebrating this beautiful feast. Pray that they might experience more fully their faith and the God we all serve. We are all bound up on this journey together, and we are called to share in the life and love of our Creator.

Finally, I'm reminded of one of the sayings used in the Passover Seder. It is custom to say, "Next year in Jerusalem," explained here from the Haggadah: "This year we are here, next year we will be in the Land of Israel.

This year we are slaves, next year we will be free."[25] The hope of our God is that we are all on a journey. This year we may be slaves, or oppressed, or marginalized, but next year, friends, we shall be free. Next year in Jerusalem!

---

25. The Haggadah is the prayerbook containing text recited during the Passover Seder.

THE GOODNESS FOUND FRIDAY

APRIL 14, 2017

I have been a columnist in this fine newspaper since 2011. I was a senior in high school (goodness, I was young) when the editor here invited me to join you on a grand adventure through the world of faith and theological thinking.

Looking back, every year I have asked what is so good about the day that Christians call Good Friday. There's much in this world to be dismally aware of: bombings in Syria, a lack of care for the poor and the disposed, a potential conflict with North Korea. These are all things that take our attention away from the goodness in the world.

Likewise, on a hill long ago there was much to be fearful about. A man was being executed as an enemy of the state in the vilest form of capital punishment developed at the time. It was as if the world had been given its best shot and the shot failed. Jesus, the one we know as Christ, was dying, soon to be dead, and we had nothing to show for it but a cross and thieves taking their last breaths.

Perhaps the goodness of this day is that it doesn't end here—that we know the rest of the story. But there are many stories in our world for which we do not know the ending. We do not know how to appropriately deal with chemical weapons in Assad's hands. We do not know how to fix the failing relationship that is on life support. We do not know how to respond to the cancer diagnosis. All these unfinished stories leave us wondering if there is such a thing as resurrection and if it could really happen to us.

Diana Butler Bass, a theologian for whom I have great respect, once reminded me that God is the unfinished sentence. I'm taking great hope in that this Good Friday, and I think you should as well.

Humanity threw the worst it had at God on Good Friday, and God retorted with Easter Sunday. But that in-between time is still dismal and hard. The liminal and transitional spaces are difficult and sometimes impossible to face.

But one of my colleagues, Dr. Emily Stone, tweeted the other day that "Liminal spaces are so, so hard but so, so holy, friend. Do not be afraid. Do not be afraid. Do not be afraid." Perhaps the goodness in Good Friday is that it's a transition, a liminal space. It does not end here.

If faced with Good Friday by itself, we would be a people most to be pitied, to borrow from the Apostle Paul (1 Cor 15:19). Or, as presiding Bishop Curry says, "If the Resurrection didn't happen, we can just go home."[26]

The hope of today is this: there is a tomorrow, and the day after that. This world will keep spinning and God will keep redeeming. We are not pitiful creatures because we have a future with hope.

This Savior of the world is already working to redeem even places like Syria and North Korea, the country club and southside Statesville. God will make right what has been tarnished, and God will restore the goodness of this day. Therein lies the Easter hope. Thanks be to God!

---

26. Sermon, Diocesan Convention, 2016.

A COLUMN TURNED PRAYER FOR ASCENSION SUNDAY

ASCENSION SUNDAY 2017

> God of grace and God of glory,
> On your people, pour thy power,
> crown thine ancient Church's story,
> bring her bud to glorious flower.
> Grant us wisdom, grant us courage,
> for the facing of this hour . . .[27]

God of the true church, we acknowledge that we know these songs we sing too well, some of them even by heart. We have committed these words to memory, and yet when it comes time to put the songs and sermons and Scripture into action, we fall strangely short in the light of your glorious plan for us.

Free us for joyful obedience so that the church might be a place where Christ is celebrated as Lord, where the poor in spirit and wealth are uplifted, where conservative and liberal and independent may worship together as an envisioning of your beloved kingdom. Where the lines we have drawn fade into the light of your glory and grace. Where the church is at the corner of social justice and personal holiness.

On this Ascension Sunday, may we be mindful that your presence will never leave us or forsake us, even if we do not have you in our physical sight. We give you thanks that you have opened the Scriptures to us this

---

27. Harry Emerson Fosdick, "God of Grace and God of Glory" (1930).

Easter season—that the Messiah must suffer, die, and rise from the dead. We give you thanks for the great fifty days of Easter and for the beauty of the queen of feasts, your glorious resurrection.

However, this day we are mindful that our world is not what it should be. Make the church be for the world the broken body and blood of your Son, so that our confidence will not be in the ballot box or politics here in Raleigh or Washington DC, but our confidence instead may be in our baptisms, in the church, and in the Spirit who gave life to the first church years ago.

Ascending Christ, you promised to send your Holy Spirit to your holy church. As you have ascended, may your Spirit descend fresh upon us. May we be bold enough to go into the world, in the strength of your Spirit, to give ourselves for others. In the name of Jesus Christ, who with you O God and the Holy Spirit, lives and reigns, one God now and forever. Amen.

PENTECOST AND THE KLAN

PENTECOST 2012

In the liturgical calendar of the church year, this Sunday is Pentecost Sunday. The feast of Pentecost is a holy day in the church that commemorates and celebrates the descent of the Holy Spirit onto the apostles of the church after Jesus' ascension. The church is to be decorated in festive reds, oranges, and yellows to symbolize the tongues of fire that were over the apostles' heads during the Pentecost experience. During this experience, which can be found in Acts 2, the apostles started speaking in different tongues.

They each heard in their "own native language": "Parthians, Medes, Elamites, and residents of Mesopotamia, Judea and Cappadocia, Pontus and Asia, Phrygia and Pamphylia, Egypt and the parts of Libya belonging to Cyrene, and visitors from Rome, both Jews and proselytes, Cretans and Arabs" (Acts 2:9-11). I bring this to your attention to point out the diversity of faith, which goes beyond just the Jewish community of the day. The grace of God was extended to everyone in attendance and beyond.

All the way in Boone, North Carolina, I have heard stories of the Ku Klux Klan meeting that will occur in Northern Iredell County tomorrow (Saturday). I would encourage each of you to be in prayer for members of this organization, that God might be at work in their lives changing, restoring, and transforming the broken nature of racism that we see.

I have been an advocate throughout my column's articles on an inclusion of love and an exclusion of hate, but it seems that some residents of the great county of Iredell feel that hate is more important than love. How do we respond? How do we fight the evil powers of this world?

We stand, together. Beyond the lines of denominationalism, nationality, race, gender, and clan, we give a resounding yes to the world's no.

Where the world says we can't, we say we can with the power of the Holy Spirit that was present those many millennia ago.

Tomorrow (Saturday), I will be praying for the people who will participate in the cross-burning. I will pray that the same grace that transformed us will transform them, so that one day the transformation in all our lives will be complete. I look to a wonderful man by the name of Martin Luther King Jr. who said so eloquently, "An individual has not started living until he can rise above the narrow confines of his individualistic concerns to the broader concerns of all humanity."[28] People of faith, that is what Pentecost is about.

Pentecost is about the life-changing act of the individual becoming the communal; it is about grapes and wheat becoming bread and wine that grace our table. Pentecost is the resounding grace that conquers the bonds and chains of racism. Pentecost is the speaking in tongues that changed the course of those apostles' lives and ever more presently changes our lives as well. In that we can say, "Thanks be to God."

---

28. *Measure of a Man* (Minneapolis: Fortress Press, 2001), 43.

WHERE WILL YOU PLACE YOUR FAITH ON ELECTION DAY?

OCTOBER 2016

This past week, my friend and I were in Washington, DC, to see the brand-new Smithsonian National Museum of African American History and Culture. As we walked through the incredible space, a sense of sadness and contemplation came over me. Some of you who are reading this article remember a time when people of color in this country were excluded by Jim Crow laws from executing their legal right to vote. This horrific injustice lays claim to a reality I've been thinking about lately: how we vote matters.

Now, you may argue that this column should speak to faith, and it does. How we vote as people of faith matters every time we go and place pen to paper on our ballots. Perhaps more than ever, this election matters for the future of this land. As a person of faith and a minister of the gospel of Jesus Christ, I am deeply concerned with the rhetoric and tone, the fear mongering and intimidation put on during this campaign season.

That being said, I am going to follow Jesus in casting my hope not on the election, not on Hillary Clinton or Donald Trump, not on Pat McCrory or Roy Cooper. There are bigger things to cast my faith on. I've prayed and voted, and now it is time for the people to decide. But God will still be God the day after the election, regardless of whether we have a President-elect Trump or a President-elect Clinton!

This is the beauty of having dual citizenship in the kingdom of God. As Stanley Hauerwas, a professor here at Duke, might put it, we are "resident aliens" living in a Christian colony here and now in this place. We didn't belong to Caesar and the Roman Empire in the first century, and we don't belong to the American Empire in the twenty-first century.

Here's my challenge to you in the week ahead: Pray for presidential candidates. Pray for gubernatorial candidates. Pray for all of those seeking elected office. Then go vote. Be a part of the system and remember that ultimately systems fail to make everyone happy. But there is a God who beckons us toward wholeness and completeness. Regardless of your party affiliation, remember this day whom you belong to. God is watching, waiting, and yearning for you to put your faith where it belongs—with Jesus Christ our Lord.

THE CHURCH, THE KINGDOM, AND ORDINARY TIME

NOVEMBER 2016

This past week, I had the wonderful opportunity to attend an end of the school year mass at St. Raphael the Archangel Catholic Church in Raleigh. I was there celebrating with a friend who was completing her studies in middle school. The beautiful service was interjected with glimpses of the kingdom of God when the kids from the school would stand up to read the prayers, litanies, and Scripture readings. As the older middle schoolers would stand up to read, they'd bring with them a much younger elementary-aged child with them to the pulpit. In this most holy moment of generational solidarity, I was able to experience the grace that keeps showing up in all of our lives.

The church is a movement of solidarity. The Reverend Dr. Samuel Wells describes solidarity this way:

> Solidarity means all the ways we seek to make concrete the intangible links between people, links based on love and trust and dignity and understanding and respect. Solidarity is what the church is called to be—Christians standing alongside one another, standing alongside the oppressed, and standing alongside God in Christ.[29]

---

29. "Solidarity: Mark 1:4-11," a sermon preached in Duke University Chapel on January 8, 2012 (chapel.duke.edu/sites/default/files/Jan8Solidarity.pdf).

At the mass we sang a hymn titled "All You Works of God." In the hymn, the hymnist describes all of us within our world as "One great song of grace and love, ever ancient, ever new."

The appropriateness of that hymn as children young and old stood together in solidarity with one another was nothing short of the future of our world in the kingdom we pray for every week during worship. To stand in solidarity with one another, across generational differences, across socio-economic limitations and racial bounds, is to glimpse what the fruition of God's work in our lives will be.

Within the liturgical calendar of our year, we're currently in the season called Ordinary Time. Many also call this season Kingdomtide. I really like that mentality; we are bound for the kingdom of God. This kingdom is one of solidarity, justice, equality, love, and grace.

One of my colleagues in ministry reminded me of the song James Taylor sings:

> Let us turn our thoughts today to Martin Luther King
> And recognize that there are ties between us
> All men and women, living on the earth
> Ties of hope and love, sister and brotherhood,
> That we are bound together
> With a desire to see the world become
> A place in which our children can grow free and strong
> We are bound together by the task that stands before us
> And the road that lies ahead, we are bound and we are bound.[30]

Friends, like those kids at St. Raphael's, we are bound together and bound for the kingdom of God. Let us stand in solidarity with one another as we proclaim God's reign as Lord of time and space. Let us finally give thanks for that glorious day of new life in which God will bring God's kingdom back to God's self. Will you help make it happen?

---

30. "Shed a Little Light," *New Moon Shine* (1991).

CHRIST THE KING SUNDAY: THE END OF THE CHURCH YEAR

NOVEMBER 2017

My wife hates spoilers; that's why she hasn't allowed me to show her one of the better episodes of *Star Trek: The Next Generation.* The final episode of the greatest television series of my life came to mind when I was geeking out with my friend Katelyn over the series. "All Good Things," parts 1 and 2, try to capture the essence of the series that defined television science fiction in the late 1980s and early 1990s.

At the end of the episode, Captain Jean Luc Picard finally sits down with his fellow officers at a poker table and begins to play the game of cards that has eluded him for so long. They remind him that he always had a seat at the table, and the episode concludes. It reminds me a little of the liturgical end of the year that we will mark this week—Christ the King Sunday.

This week, after all is said and done with turkey and stuffing, we will gather in worshiping communities across this country and proclaim that Christ has a seat at the table, and that for us the incarnation is the heart of the Advent journey we are about to embark on. The fact that God would get down and become one of us in the fruition of time and space long ago is the most convincing and convicting act a deity could take. But God, like the captain of the starship *Enterprise,* chose to be *with* people instead of above us. God broke down the barrier that separates humankind from God, and that is a great gift.

Christ the King Sunday, Advent, and Christmas—for me these seasonal and liturgical markers are where I learn to believe again. Where I learn that God in God's goodness became like us. The incarnation allows us to circle around in the liturgical year and enthrone Christ as king of our lives. It allows us to enter into a soteriology of hope instead of fear. We are free to believe in an incarnate Christ instead of a condemning Christ.

That's where so many faith leaders get it wrong these days. Christ came not to condemn but to enter into a blessed relationship. God comes and sits at the table with us. That's the goodness of the season. May we crown God as Lord of our lives, as Lord of time and space, and as the hope of the world. Therein we will find new beginnings at the end of the liturgical year. Cheers to the end of this liturgical year, and blessings in the Advent to come.

ON THE ANNIVERSARY OF A TRAGEDY (SEPTEMBER 11, 2001)

SEPTEMBER 11, 2013

I want to share with you a little-known story about the book of Jeremiah in the Old Testament. Jeremiah had a devoted friend and secretary named Baruch ben Neriah, who faithfully recorded the prophet's words and prophecies. One of my favorite stories from Jeremiah comes when Baruch is commanded by Jeremiah to go to the temple and read the prophecies, because Jeremiah cannot perform this duty due to the wrath of the king. Baruch does so without question or fear.

You might be wondering what this has to do with the context in which our world is turning this weekend. Granted, many columnists, pundits, and all of the media will be turning their eyes to the past and to Ground Zero as we remember the horrible events of September 11, 2001. I want to propose a question this day that seeks to look to the future of humanity in a post 9-11 world.

Where will we as a society be fifty years from now? Will we still be searching for answers to our questions surrounding the fateful day of September 11? Will we still be consumed with anger and fear a century from now, when most of us will be long gone? Where will we be? I ask these questions, for they are questions that deserve answers.

You see, I believe in the God of redemption. A God that can redeem even the most horrifying event, the crucifixion. A God whose heart hurt not only on September 11 but still hurts today as genocide rages and people go hungry. I believe in the God of the ages, who has stood the test of time.

There's a wonderful hymn that goes like this: "God of love and God of power, thou hast called us for this hour."[31] We have been called by God to be witnesses to the redemption, witnesses to the newness of grace. The best thing we as people of faith can do this weekend is be like Baruch and share our stories. Stories of that day, not of terror but of that hope that came from the rubble. We should not be afraid of the consequences and what our stories mean to others. We should be hopeful in the potential our stories have to change the course of time. You see, Baruch wasn't afraid of the story, and we shouldn't be either; the context of our faith is that we are called to be storytellers of the gospel of our lives. We are to share the gospel through our actions and our stories.

September 11, 2001, will never be forgotten, and rightfully so. Our stories will continue until they are woven into the great chain of time. Then, when our stories are complete, we will see the redemption of our stories. We will see the redemption of the horror caused that day. Then, in God's almighty power, there will be peace.

---

31. Gerald Kennedy, "God of Love and God of Power" (c. 1939).

ISSUES OF CONSEQUENCE AND FAITH

But he's already made it plain how to live, what to do, what God is looking for in men and women. It's quite simple: Do what is fair and just to your neighbor, be compassionate and loyal in your love, and don't take yourself too seriously—take God seriously.

—*Micah 6:8* (The Message)

Statesville is a beautiful town, but I am very unlike many of my fellow citizens in my theological and political views. That said, these articles attempt to bridge a divide of difference for a community torn apart and polarized by our current climate. Whether we like it or not, we are forced to reckon with our own views and share them with others. Here is my attempt.

"BUILDING A BRIDGE": AN INTERVIEW WITH FATHER JAMES MARTIN

OCTOBER 12, 2017

He might be the most famous Catholic priest in the country. Father James Martin, SJ, has sat down with me before, and I consider him to be a light in this world. But this past year he, like me, has faced controversy. He wrote a book titled *Building a Bridge: How the Catholic Church Can Enter into a Relationship of Respect, Compassion, and Sensitivity*. I sat down with Father Martin and interviewed him about his new book and his hopes for our world.

Question: *You've made headlines lately for what some Christians characterize as holy reasons and what others characterize as heretical reasons. Why are Christians so divided?*

James Martin: On the issue of welcoming LGBT people? There's probably a combination of reasons for the opposition to what I'm proposing in my book. First and foremost, homophobia, the fear of the LGBT person as the "other"—that is, actual fear. Then there is homophobia in the more colloquial sense: hatred of LGBT people. Finally, there is the fear of one's own complicated sexuality, which manifests itself in rage. But what I'm calling for in my book is pretty mild: "respect, compassion, and sensitivity" for LGBT people in our churches. It's pretty surprising that even that is too much for some Christians. If respect is heretical, then we've misread the Gospels.

Q: What would Jesus say about what you call the "consistent ethic of life"? That is to say, how do we engage the gospel from conception to grave?

JM: Jesus himself practiced a "consistent ethic of life" in his public ministry. He treated all human life as sacred. Think of all the people whose lives were considered somehow "less than," especially the sick, in Jesus' time. Our Lord treated them with the greatest of respect and care. For me the "consistent ethic of life," or the "seamless garment approach," reminds us that all life—from natural conception to natural death—is to be reverenced. All life is a sacred and precious gift from God. That includes the life of the unborn but also the life of the refugee, the migrant, the unwed mother, the person with a terminal illness, as well as the life of the ill-clothed homeless person, the struggling single parent, and the bullied LGBT teen. All life is sacred.

Q: Steve Bannon recently cited undocumented immigrants and the church's need to fill pews.[32] With that in mind, what is the church's mission to people within our borders who are undocumented?

JM: It is Jesus' mission, as elaborated in Matthew 25, to welcome the stranger. There are many things in the Gospels that may be difficult to interpret, or at least open to interpretation, but this passage couldn't be any clearer. When you welcome the stranger, you welcome Jesus himself. And, by the way, if you also add the parable of the good Samaritan, we're reminded that Jesus doesn't say welcome the stranger only when it's easy, or only when it's convenient, or only when he's from the same ethnic group, or only when there's no danger involved. He says, "Welcome them." Remember, in the case of the good Samaritan, the Samaritan incurs significant risk when he helps the man. After all, the man has been beaten and robbed along a dangerous stretch of road. So we are called to welcome the stranger. Period.

Q: Your newest book speaks of building a bridge between the church and the LGBTQ community. What has been your takeaway from this journey of writing and the backlash you've received since its release?

JM: My takeaway is that the passionate reactions on both sides show that the book needed to be written. The overwhelming response has been positive.

---

32. Alana Abramson, "Steve Bannon: Bishops Support the Undocumented So They Can Fill Pews," *Time*, September 20, 2017 (time.com/4931496/steve-bannon-daca-catholic-church-60-minutes/).

When I give talks at parishes or retreat houses or conferences, people come up to hug me or cry when they say how much they appreciate the book. And I've been overwhelmed by the letters, cards, emails, and conversations with people expressing support and encouragement. My sense is that even though the book is mild, and doesn't challenge any church teaching, LGBT people and their families are grateful for the call for welcome and inclusion, particularly coming from a priest. On the other side, some of the frankly hysterical responses from hateful far-right online sites and magazines show how much homophobia there still is in the church. So both responses indicate that the book needed to be written.

RL: *If you have one piece of advice to church communities in a small town like Statesville, what might that be?*
JM: Welcome people who seem different from you. Just consider the Gospels. When Jesus reaches out to people who feel like they are on the margins, he leads first with welcome, not condemnation. He doesn't shout, "Sinner" or "Pagan"! Rather, he welcomes first. So "Love one another" in many cases means "Welcome one another."

PEACE WITH JUSTICE

SEPTEMBER 2019

When I picture what God looks like, I picture Bertha Hamilton. Mrs. Bertha has worked with my mother for some thirty years and was my confirmation mentor. Mrs. Bertha is also a person of color and has deeply influenced the way I look at race and the cost of discipleship. She is a humble servant and someone in whom I see the face of God whenever I am with her.

I never fully understood Dietrich Bonhoeffer's term "cheap grace" until these past weeks. You see, I bear the name Robert Lee, and I am a descendant of the Confederate general who led the army against this nation for states' rights to own slaves. I had the opportunity to speak up and speak out after recent riots surrounding the preservation of a memorial to General Lee in Charlottesville, Virginia.[33] On August 27, I appeared on the MTV Video Music Awards with the mother of the late Heather Heyer, a young woman who was killed when a car drove into a crowd of counter-protestors. The hate I have received has been surreal and pernicious. The threats I have received inconceivable. But it all reminded me that Christians are easily tempted by cheap grace.

I'm positive Jesus would have called out the message boards and angry tweets if they were around when Matthew 18 was occurring. Jesus is clear how to handle disputes, disagreements, and anger in the church. But it seems to me that many of our parishioners and clergy glance over this reality for the sake of "righteous" zeal.

It concerns me that I was told my appearance on the Video Music Awards and my speaking up that black lives matter was enough for Christians to come unhinged and want to confront me. Some Christians have

---

33. Andrew Katz, "Unrest in Virginia: Clashes over a Show of White Nationalism in Charlottesville Turn Deadly," *Time* (time.comcharlottesville-white-nationalist-rally-clashes/).

become so blind to hate that they have forgotten the importance of Matthew 18 conversations.

I've been told I sold my soul, that I am not to be celebrated, and that there is a place in hell that belongs to me. Does that sound like how Christ envisioned confronting conflict and discord amid followers of the Way? Ultimately, we're all in this together. No wonder people say Christianity just isn't worth it anymore. The discord of our infighting has drowned out the sweet sound of grace.

Please don't hear me as bemoaning the institutional church. I love it deeply. But the cracks are widening as we face down these issues that divide us. Evangelicals and mainline Protestants rarely come to the table together anymore; we're so locked off to each other that we can't converse. This has also played out in the realm of LGBTQ+ rights. The recent Nashville Statement made by a majority of white men is enough to make one's skin crawl.[34] I've been saddened that we can't even talk anymore. We're forced to issue our own statements in response or to write think pieces about how bad we've become.

I am convinced that the heart of the gospel falls nearer to love and reconciliation than it does to statements, hate messages, and Confederate monuments. So why does it seem that the loudest Christians on the block are issuing statements, conferring hate, and seeking the safety of idolatrous monuments?

Ezekiel makes it clear that we can change. We don't have to live this way. In my own mainline tradition, I want to scream that if we don't speak up now, we will lose everything we hold dear. For mainline Protestants, we have to speak up and speak out in the name of the God we have come to know. Because Matthew 18 leaves us with great hope: "Where two or more are gathered in my name, I am among them."

We might lose everything speaking up, but we will gain so much more when we decide the time is now. We may forfeit everything for standing on the side of justice, but that sounds a lot more like the way of Jesus than erecting or defending monuments and the Nashville Statement. The hope of this text is that in losing your life by being with people, you will gain the promise and assurance of abundance.

---

34. "Thousands of Christians Respond to Nashville Statement with Emphatic 'No,'" *Sojourners*, August 31, 2017 (sojo.net/articles/thousands-christians-respond-nashville-statement-emphatic-no).

It's my prayer that the loudest voice in the room will become the voice of sanity. That the voice is a collective voice that can only come from a gathering of people humbled before God's love and not from a Facebook post gone viral.

This is the greatest hope we have, that we are not alone and we can face each other with dignity and respect. This way of thinking shifts the focus of our faith from internal to external, from institutional to missional. To borrow from Dr. King, none of us know what will happen to us, but we've been to the mountaintop and seen what's around the bend. It is costly grace that will lead us home into the very heart of God in which we all dwell together. Cheap grace will divide us as the lure of acceptance without repentance turns us inward to only forgive and to sanction what is most familiar while rejecting those whom are cast outside our circle of care.

If we do the hard work of reconciliation, God will be there.

So keep the faith. When you gather for worship and seek the heart of God you will find it, but you must be prepared because the heart of God is not a white male's view of the world. As troubling as that is for the world, we must see it for ourselves. We should hope beyond hope that God will reconcile the most privileged of us to God's self. We don't deserve it because God is the god of the lowly. But I am confident that if we do the hard work of reconciliation, God will be there.

Mrs. Bertha may never fully understand the fullness of what she means to me and countless others, but I know my image of God is not complete without her. So look for the people who exemplify God and a Matthew 18 way of doing things. Cling to the people for whom God is not distant but close at hand. Seek the people who, when you are with them, you know the face of God.

FACING MENTAL ILLNESS WITH FAITH

MAY 2015

I suffer from a mental illness. At times, it can be crippling and debilitating. I just spent six days in the hospital dealing with my illness. One of the doctors knew I am a divinity student and Christian minister, and he asked me as he was treating me, "Have you lost your faith?" I held back tears as I said that no, I hadn't lost my faith, but I was acutely aware that perhaps that wasn't always the case for every patient the doctor saw.

How odd of God to call a mentally ill person to Christian ministry, but maybe God is a little crazy. Actually, God must be crazy. How odd of God to call humanity to be better and more in tune with God's self. But God being crazy is precisely what makes God identifiable to some. God is just crazy enough to be real, and frankly some of us need a crazy God to keep us sane. Some of us facing mental health issues need to roll away the stone of mental illness and claim the resurrecting power of vulnerability and authenticity.

I'm hoping people of faith will read this and be honest with themselves, their families, friends, and places of worship and admit that mental illness is scary, but God is a big God. God hung the earth upon the waters, and if the lilies can be cared for, if God's eye is on the sparrow, then what have we to fret?[35] Certainly it is easier said than done, but perhaps we are to a point where we must throw everything we have at mental illness, including the God we serve, because God is a powerful ally.

I'm not suggesting we shouldn't seek treatment, medication, or therapy; it's actually quite the opposite. By the grace of God, we are given these tools to fight mental illness. What I am suggesting is that we claim the promise

---

35. Matt 6:28; 10:20-31.

made in Scripture that God would never leave us or forsake us. Regardless of whether we are in the bowels of mental illness or in a hospital room, regardless of whether we've had a mental health issue yesterday or thirty years ago, we are to claim the promise that while it may not be easy, we are not alone.

Someone in the hospital pushed me to ask if God did this to me. I don't think that's the God I have come to know, but I know this: I have never felt closer to God than when I'm fighting mental illness or advocating for my mental health. That is because God is just crazy enough to love someone like me, and, frankly, that is the good news. Our faith is confidence that we are loved and can love others. As the hymn goes, "The task looms large before us, the cry goes up how long, and soon the night of weeping shall be the morn of song."[36]

---

36. S. J. Stone, "The Church's One Foundation" (1866).

ORLANDO, LITURGY, AND ACTION

JUNE 14, 2016

I'm doing my field education at a large downtown Methodist church in Raleigh, North Carolina. Normally, waking up early on the first day of the week while it is still dark should be a joyous work for pastors and church staff. But early this past Sunday, news started to come in of a mass shooting in Orlando.[37] The number of fatalities kept rising, and I realized in that moment that we at the church I serve had a choice to make: do we alter our liturgy for the morning to acknowledge and pray for the horrific events, or do we go on with business as usual? The choice for me and for my field education mentor was clear: we had to say something. We had to mark the atrocious acts of a terrorist on our LGBTQ brothers and sisters. It was not the time to talk about polity or what the United Methodist Church believes is compatible or incompatible with Christian teaching; it was time to do what the church has done for centuries prior. It was time to pray.

The first hymn played at our 11:00am service. We had three baptisms right after the processional hymn, but I asked our congregation to be seated and noted we would be changing the liturgy of the service. If liturgy really is the work of the people as we believe it to be, it was time for us to give voice to what we were undoubtedly feeling. We challenged each other to pray and let our prayers be turned to action. We acknowledged that there was a time for the heartbreak and horror our community members were feeling. We said that though there was a time for heartbreak and horror, we hoped that it would turn to action, to a day when we beat our swords

---

37. Ariel Zambelich and Alyson Hurt, "3 Hours in Orlando: Piecing Together an Attack and Its Aftermath," *The Two Way*, NPR.com, June 26, 2016 (npr.org/2016/06/16/482322488/orlando-shooting-what-happened-update).

into plowshares and our spears into pruning hooks and we train for war no more.[38]

I tell you this because today, this week, this month, the larger community will be watching what the church does in these moments. Will we offer thoughts and prayers today and condemnation the next day? Will we say we will change our tune on gun violence and then go back to the same status quo that got us here in the first place?

May our liturgy be bold enough to proclaim the good news of Jesus Christ, news that demands of us action and resolve. May we be the agents of change through our liturgy, polity, and community action. Let us hold each other accountable when anti-LGBT rhetoric is communicated; after all, in my tradition in our baptisms, we are called to "resist evil and oppression in whatever forms they present themselves." Well, people, now is the time to resist and to act. May our liturgy reflect the sure and certain reality that God will use us to make things right.

---

38. Isa 2:4.

BE STRONG AND COURAGEOUS

MARCH 6, 2015

Have you read the story in the first chapter of the book of Joshua? Moses had just died and now Joshua, son of Nun—Moses' assistant—was in charge of the entire nation of Israel. It would be his responsibility to lead them into the land promised to the Israelites since before he was born. As Joshua prepares for this holy and daunting mission, God commands him in verse 9, "I hereby command you: Be strong and courageous; do not be frightened or dismayed, for the LORD your God is with you wherever you go.'"

Courage. It's often a tenet of our faith that is easily overlooked amid myriad other things we're supposed to remember. Courage doesn't come up until we have that big job interview, or perhaps the cancer has returned, or maybe there's a funeral that we weren't prepared for. By that point, it may be too late to be courageous in the faith. So let me offer you three ideas of how we might practice courage in our daily lives.

1. Part of courage is staying far away from discouragement; in reality, discouragement is the antithesis of courage. It brings you down and prevents you from having courage. Maybe you didn't get that job, or maybe your parents are sick. In those situations, it's easy to get discouraged. But courage isn't ignoring discouragement. It's learning to deal with it and preventing it from controlling you.

2. Courage takes practice. Courage means you remember that you belong to God, that God is on your side, and that God goes with you wherever you go. God is for you, and if God is for you, who can be against

you?[39] The battle has already been won, and now we have the responsibility to be courageous enough to celebrate that victory.

3. Finally, let your courage speak to others and encourage them to be courageous as well. Your courage gives others permission to be courageous. You become the hands and feet of Christ on this terrestrial sphere. You are God's agent of change in the face of a daunting moment; you are God's best hope to enable others to be courageous too.

Dear people of God, you are beloved. You have permission to be courageous in any situation because the Lord your God is with you just as God was with Joshua in the days of old. May you experience grace this week with whatever situation you are facing. May God uplift you and enable you to stand and face the future with hope. For in the hope of a better future is where courage lies. Thanks be to God!

---

39. Rom 8:31.

EDUCATION IS A FAITH ISSUE

AUGUST 4, 2017

School starts back soon, and my friend Molly Wright visited Stephanie and me in Boone this week. She has been a dear friend since high school, when she was the cool senior who gave me (the lowly freshman) rides home in her Jeep Cherokee, all while listening to the coolest music I have ever heard. We reminisced about times gone by and looked to the future: Molly is a teacher, a graduate of North Carolina State University, and has enrolled in Harvard University's extension master's program in education.

I asked her why she was doing this program and why it mattered now. She said in sure and certain terms that the children she was teaching needed a chance and attention that people are neglecting to give them. She believes, as many educators do, that she can make a difference in young people's lives the same way people like Wanda McConnell did for us when we were in high school English class at Statesville High School. But that answer, for me at least, made education a faith issue.

Now mind you, I am not advocating prayer in schools or the implementation of religious education; that is the job of families and churches. What I am saying is that people of faith in Statesville should be deeply concerned with the education our students are getting in our community. This call to action comes just weeks after a young person was shot down in our community, and it prompts the question: What more can we do with our systems and institutions so something like this never, ever happens again?

The reality is that if we're going to change this old world, we must do it through institutions and systems that have worked in the past but may need tweaking now. We must be like my friend Molly and engage in the hard work of reconciliation and education for the sake of our future. If we're willing to be people who do this together, there is nothing that can stop Statesville.

To all the educators out there, from Molly Wright to Wanda McConnell, you are valued, and you are cherished. You have made a difference and continue to do so by your presence in the lives of our young people. You change the course of our collective history by your actions, and I can promise my prayers go with you. I challenge my readers to pray the same prayer I am praying. I have included it below. May God help us to educate and to reconcile, for in those two words we see our future.

God, in our ever-renewing love for us, you gave us educators and teachers. Grant that in your gracious hope for our lives together, your teachers may be renewed in strength and reconciliation toward the students in our community. May we see the dawn of a new tomorrow in our education system. For the sake of your name, we pray. Amen.

INTERVIEW: THEOLOGIAN AND THINKER DIANA BUTLER BASS

JANUARY 26, 2017

Diana Butler Bass is a well-known Protestant theologian and scholar. She has written nine books and has preached and lectured in small churches and in the National Cathedral. She has taught at universities and received numerous awards, but now she considers herself an independent scholar of theology, religion, and culture.

It was my privilege to sit down with Dr. Butler Bass and hear what she has to say about what's going on in our world. I just finished rereading her 2015 book *Grounded*, which comes out in paperback next month. I highly recommend it to you all.

Question: *What gives you hope?*
Diana Butler Bass: My garden. The local farmers' market. A beautiful Celtic evening service at a church in Richmond, Virginia (I sometimes drive the ninety minutes from my home near Washington just to attend). My family and friends, who are edgy and honest and smart and passionate. I was at the Women's March in Washington on January 21. Hundreds of thousands of women in the streets—grandmothers, moms, kids; black, brown, white, Asian; all different religions. It gave me hope.

There was a lovely thing in that march, one not reported in the news because it was a small thing. I met up with a group of friends, most of whom are clergy. For hours, we stood on some rocks right outside the American Indian Museum and held up signs with the Beatitudes on them. People marched by and cheered the Beatitudes. Yes: they cheered the Beatitudes.

Many stopped and wanted someone to pray with or for them. The whole thing gave me a fresh vision of Jesus and the Sermon on the Mount. Jesus on that hill proclaiming truth: "Blessed are the poor; blessed are the immigrants; blessed are the outcasts; blessed are those who mourn." That is what it means to be Christian—to hold up the Beatitudes to the crowd and invite people to a life shaped by love. It was powerful.

Q: What spiritual practices are meaningful for you? What do those spiritual practices look like in the twenty-first century?
DBB: Silence. I sometimes attend a silent Quaker meeting these days. The world is so noisy. Silence is a necessary corrective. And I'm exploring different practices of gratitude—like waking up and saying "thank you" first thing in the morning and saying the same last thing before bed. Putting a gratitude "frame" around the day. Engaging strangers in conversation wherever I go. People are lonely. And I consider it a spiritual practice to reach out. Sometimes I'm rebuffed. But mostly I'm amazed at how much people want to share with strangers about things that matter. Listening to people who are not white. I'm reading more books, watching films, and engaging social media from the black community. Trying to hear non-defensively and learn from my brothers and sisters. Oh, and I'm reading much more of the Hebrew Bible than ever before. I needed a new lens into Scripture and am finding the Old Testament profoundly meaningful, especially when I discuss it with Jewish friends.

I don't think any of those things are unique to the twenty-first century—silence, gratitude, welcoming strangers, listening and discernment, reading Scripture. The list seems in line with classical spiritual practices in Christianity and in other religions. But the context is so different now. The context heightens the significance and urgency of all these practices.

Q: I loved your statement on a recent podcast I heard that "God is the unfinished sentence." Could you speak to that? What does that mean for Christians today?
DBB: I'm a writer. And there is a moment when you know that the word is just beyond what you can put on paper—that the word is elusive, mysterious, healing, pregnant with truth and meaning. The unfinished sentence. And that's how I think of God these days. That Word hovering right beyond our capacity to know—the shimmer of truth that is always calling us toward completion.

I know what it means for me. That God is both with us here and now, the active presence of love in and through all things. But that God is always just beyond as well. The Word pulling us toward deeper words. This vision plunges me into wonder, into a sense that I must keep writing the life of faith, that nothing is completed yet. The story still calls.

Q: Finally, tell us about your new edition of your book, Grounded.
DBB: The paperback releases on February 14 [2017]. We added a forty-day devotional in the back of the book so readers can "pray through" the chapters as they read, giving people a sort of "lectio divina" (holy reading) approach to it. I originally wrote the devotional on Facebook—one devotion for each day of Lent last year. My Facebook friends loved it. It is suitable for Lent—or for anytime one chooses a forty-day prayer practice.

TO GET TO HEAVEN, YOU HAVE TO KNOW YOUR GEOGRAPHY

APRIL 7, 2017

This past week, Duke University Divinity School's Office of Black Church Studies sponsored its annual Distinguished Martin Luther King Jr. Lecture here at the divinity school.

The Rev. Dr. Marvin McMickle was the guest lecturer, and he preached a rousing sermon on Acts 1:6-8, which says "So when they had come together, they asked him, 'Lord, is this the time when you will restore the kingdom to Israel?' He replied, 'It is not for you to know the times or periods that the Father has set by his own authority. But you will receive power when the Holy Spirit has come upon you; and you will be my witnesses in Jerusalem in all Judea and Samaria, and to the ends of the earth.'" During his sermon, Dr. McMickle remarked, "To get to heaven, you have to go through Samaria, the place you do not want to go."

What a statement to make! But I think it warrants some context. Samaria was most certainly a place where Jesus' first disciples did not want to go. The Samaritans were religiously and ethically unclean in the eyes of the Jews. They were "those people" of their time. They were the people you didn't associate with; they lived on the other side of the proverbial train tracks. They were the kids your parents told you not to play with.

So to get to heaven, you have to know geography. You have to know where God is calling you to go. And I echo Dr. McMickle: You cannot get to heaven without going through your own Samaria. You cannot get to heaven without reaching out to south Statesville, or the country club, or the other corner of Center Street, or, dare I even say, Mooresville. Whatever "those people" are for you, you must go to them and proclaim the life-changing, earth-shattering love of Jesus Christ.

Let me be clear: heaven is not segregated based on your personal tastes and sensibilities. So if you have a problem with other people of faith, you better start getting used to the idea of an eternity with them. This is a hard pill to swallow, but if we're bound for the kingdom of God we're going to have to go there together. If geography, race, socioeconomic level, sexual or gender identity, ethnic identity, or any other identity scare you out of befriending "those people" (who very well might be Christians themselves), then you're not doing this following Jesus thing right.

If Jesus really is the Christ, and the resurrection and Pentecost really did happen, we can trust my favorite of Paul's words found in Galatians: "There is no longer Jew or Greek, there is no longer slave or free, there is no longer male and female; for all of you are one in Christ Jesus" (3:28). If we are one in the Spirit of Christ, then nothing can stop this church of God from doing great things in the world.

So press on, brothers and sisters! Go on to south Statesville, go on to the country club, go down to the far corners of Center Street, go even to Mooresville—and find God there. For if you want to get to heaven, if you want to see God for yourself, you have to know geography.

DISEASE OF ADDICTION MUST BE ADDRESSED BY FAITH COMMUNITY

JUNE 30, 2016

In the United Church of Canada, there is an affirmation of faith that says, "In life, in death, in life beyond death, we are not alone." Jenn Kline has lived that reality with the story of her brother.

When you first meet Jenn, you would think she's a caring and considerate student at Appalachian State University. She's studying to get her master's in clinical mental health counseling, and her smile does a great job of masking the pain she feels.

February 8, 2015, sticks in her mind, and frankly in my mind as well. I can tell you where I was when my fiancée got the call from Jenn that her brother, Jake, had overdosed on heroin and died after a lengthy struggle with opiate addiction. I sat down with Jenn and we talked about her brother's addiction, and I think it's important because addiction is something that permeates our faith communities. We as people of faith are not immune to the disease of addiction, and we must address it faithfully and honestly. It's become a huge issue in our nation, and it needs to be talked about.

When I spoke with Jenn, I asked her where she saw God in these moments of dealing with her brother's addiction and death. She spoke of her hope of sharing about her brother's addiction and how it might lead people toward acceptance of their own realities. She said these words as a means of finding God:

> My forced relationship with death has made me a more spiritual person. A path has been created for me and continues to unfold in

front of my eyes. Through death you find beauty in every moment, and every sound, taste, and feeling. You find beauty within yourself. A higher power has without a doubt placed itself in front of me. My brother's death didn't "happen for a reason," yet in a way I feel his soul is able to help even more people from the beyond. Ultimately, through my brother's death has come my purpose. The beauty in my life now comes from the continuing opportunity to share my brother's story to help others.

Jenn's story is one that is unique in circumstance but all too real for millions of Americans who struggle with addiction or have a family member who has suffered from the disease. Why is this a faith issue, you might ask. The person of Jesus Christ, that first-century Palestinian Jewish rabbi whom we have come to know as Lord, spoke of caring for those who are sick, and I don't read of any distinctions Jesus made between physical and mental health. Though the disease of addiction leaves few physical scars, our faith communities must be open and honest about what it means to care for someone with this illness. We must be willing to stand in the gap and point them to professional help.

As you go throughout your week, pray for those who struggle with addiction. Then, let your prayers be turned to action as you go forth to be the person God created you to be, someone who cares for those who are hurting with the pain of addiction. I asked Jenn what she might say to someone who is struggling with addiction, and this was her response: "We are here for you, and we care. There is no need to feel guilt or be ashamed. The conversation has started, and people are beginning to listen. Have faith and stay strong. You are not alone."

GOD IS NOT DONE WITH US YET

DECEMBER 24, 2015

My friend the Rev. Nathan Kirkpatrick was ordained an Episcopal priest this past Sunday. I've been lucky enough to know Nathan for almost a decade now, and he has become one of my greatest mentors and closest friends. He preached at my ordination service at First Baptist Church in West Jefferson, and to this day I still remember what he said and what he meant by it. Nathan preached so eloquently: "Every time we ordain someone to ministry, it is a sign that God is not done with us yet."

I wonder what signs and symbols point you to the reality that God is not done with you yet. Could it be a friend like Nathan, your spouse, your church, your volunteer work? What have you seen this season that has taught you to believe again?

You see, I'm of a mindset that we don't always receive the glorious fruits of salvation in one blinding moment (though it may come in that form); instead, we receive saving grace every moment we see the works of God in the world. So this Christmas Day, as you are reading this, what has taught you to believe once more? What has kindled the fire of the incarnation we celebrate this day in you?

I want to add to Nathan's statement, if I may. Every time we lift our candles and receive Communion on Christmas Eve, every time we draw close to family members and friends this holiday season, it is a sign that God is not done with the world yet. The reality is for me and countless others: we hold fast to the hope of a resurrecting God. A God who loved us so much that God became one of us and walked among us. The Word became flesh, as John's Gospel says.

There's an old saying that I hold fast to this time of year: "God has not brought you this far to leave you alone." God is not done with the world.

The hopes and fears of all the years are met in God this day. The dawn of redeeming grace is upon us, and now it's time to start acting like it.

When the bishop laid her hands upon Nathan and ordained him a priest and commissioned him to share the good news of Jesus Christ, I thought of the work we are all called to do this season. We are called to touch, to hold, to share the gospel of our Lord as if the world depended on it. And here's a little secret: the world does indeed depend on it. So why are you waiting? Go forth into the world knowing that God goes with you. Joy to the world, the Lord has come.

GOD IS GLORIFIED THROUGH MUSIC

SEPTEMBER 5, 2014

My little brother Scott is attending the University of North Carolina School of the Arts. The other night we went to hear one of his professors perform a recital. It got me thinking about the music we adorn our worship with every Sunday.

Read these lyrics from one of the best hymns our church has: "When in our music God is glorified, and adoration leaves no room for pride, it is as though the whole creation cried alleluia! How often, making music, we have found a new dimension in the world of sound, as worship moved us to a more profound alleluia!"[40]

To worship God in music is to add a dimension to our lives. It allows for us to create a sound pleasing to our ears but also to God's. Like the ancient people lifted sacrifices to God above, we too raise our voices in liturgy and song. John Wesley, the brother of great hymn-writer Charles Wesley, proclaimed, "I'll praise my maker while I've breath!"[41] We praise God all the days of our lives through varied ways because ultimately that is what we're called to do.

The next time you are in worship, remember the beauty of the hymns you sing. Even though some of them may be old, their message rings true today. I have a special affinity for hymns, but whatever your style of worship, there is beauty in singing to the God who created you.

---

40. Fred Pratt Green, "When in Our Music God Is Glorified" (1971).

41. "History of Hymns: Watts' 'Praise My Maker' among Wesley's favorites," UMC Discipleship.org, May 21, 2013 (umcdiscipleship.org/resources/history-of-hymns-watts-praise-my-maker-among-wesleys-favorites).

When you sing a hymn or spiritual song, concentrate on the words, the melody, and the harmonies created by those who surround you. Keep in mind your own place in that setting and how God is recreating you and restoring you in those moments. Keep watch for how God might be doing that in other people's lives. You never know; you'd be surprised by what God does in your life through music.

MAKE WELCOME THE REFUGEE IN YOUR MIDST

NOVEMBER 25, 2015

As you are reading this, you are undoubtedly coming out of a turkey-induced coma and preparing for a day of madness at the mall, decorating the house, or simply recovering from having so much family gathered around the table for a meal.

I thought of writing about the perils of consumerism or the dangers of taking things for granted on this Black Friday. But instead I want to speak to something heavy on my heart.

Throughout these past weeks, there has been considerable phobia surrounding the refugee in our midst. Governors have been "banning" refugees from their states, Congress took up a bill to create even stricter regulatory measures surrounding those who need help, and Facebook has been aglow with people giving their opinion on the matter.[42]

I'm not here to start a political conversation. I'm here to remind us of our faith. Jesus himself was a refugee in Egypt after his birth. And, as we begin to celebrate the Advent of our Lord, may we be reminded of that detail often glanced over on our way to bigger and better things in Scripture.

Deeper than that, I challenge you to read the genealogy of Jesus found in Matthew 1:1-17. If you read it, you will see that those who played the greatest role in the story of Jesus weren't characters with upstanding

---

42. Ariel Seipel, "30 Governors Call for Halt to U.S. Resettlement of Syrian Refugees," NPR.com, November 17, 2015 (npr.org/2015/11/17/456336432/more-governors-oppose-u-s-resettlement-of-syrian-refugees); Megan Cassella and Patricia Zengerle, "House Passes Bill to Slow Syrian Refugees despite Obama Veto Threat," Reuters.com, November 19, 2015 (reuters.com/article/us-paris-shooting-congress/house-passes-bill-to-slow-syrian-refugees-despite-obama-veto-threat-idUSKCN0T82PG20151120).

credentials; they were refugees (Abraham and Ruth), they were sinners with a past (David), and one was even a prostitute from Jericho (Rahab).

What I am trying to say here is that the story of redemption is for the last and least of these. This Christmas story that we celebrate was built on the backs of those whom society wouldn't welcome today. So in your shopping and in your preparing, may you remember those whom Jesus welcomed into his lineage, and remember the people we should welcome too.

The reality is that we aren't people of prestige who have the power to change the lives of thousands of refugees in far-off lands. But we are people who have power and privilege to welcome those in our midst here in Statesville, here in North Carolina. Think of the lives we could change!

I am reminded of the story of the monastery that was failing miserably. In desperation, the head of the monastery went out in the woods to an old hut where a rabbi lived. He asked the rabbi how he might save the monastery. The rabbi replied, "Take heart. The Messiah is in your midst, but you do not know who it is." The head of the monastery, taking this literally, ran back to the monastery and declared to the monks, "One of us is the Messiah! But I do not know who it is."

Suddenly the monks changed their tune and started to treat each other differently. They treated each other with dignity and respect, as if they might be the Messiah in their midst. Their numbers grew, and their monastery was saved. The point of this story is to illustrate that you never know who is in your midst. You never know; you may be entertaining angels unaware.[43]

So take heart, and welcome those who do not know what it's like to have a seat at the table of grace, for the Messiah is coming. Are you ready?

---

43. Heb 13:2.

PRACTICE YOUR BUSINESS FAITHFULLY

JUNE 18, 2015

Recently, there's been a multitude of headlines surrounding Christian business practices and what it means to offer services to people who might be what some would consider atypical.

People are banning other people from stores, moving to different banks because of policies, and trying a variety of other tactics to supposedly keep them grounded in their faith. While this may seem harmless, many well-meaning people of faith can do a lot of harm by how they act, so I'd like to provide two examples of what true, faith-filled business transactions can look like.

As I mentioned in [an earlier] article, I was in a car accident that left me stranded and without a car. So in the course of the past few weeks, I have been car shopping. This led me throughout this great western part of the state searching for the right fit for me. I finally landed with a salesman named Oscar here in Statesville.

I'm not sure of Oscar's faith; we never really talked about it. But I am sure his witness to me and to my family as we talked out all our options was nothing short of Christ-like. The realities of buying a car can be daunting, but Oscar handled it with honesty and kindness.

I also think of Danny at a store in the mall here in Statesville. His willingness to help or to make me laugh continues to keep me centered and help me remember the joy that should happen when someone is buying something exciting and cool.

I'm simply giving these examples to say that you don't have to ban people from stores, as some in the news have, to keep your faith intact. You simply play your part as a follower of God and the rest will fall into place.

We are called to be in this world for whatever time we are allotted, so we might as well embrace the world for the beauty it has.

So the next time you are faced with a business choice or practice, face it with your Christ-like example and respect for human dignity. For all of us are made in the image of God, and likewise we should all be treated as such. I'm thankful for the example that Oscar and Danny can give us regarding our faith in action, and I hope we can learn that whatever we do, we should do so in love.

GIVE FAITHFULLY TO THE WORK OF GOD

APRIL 17, 2015

I don't know about you, but anytime I hear the words, "Would you prayerfully consider giving?" I automatically turn off my ears. In many unhealthy cases, those words are considered to be begging for money from churches and missions to meet the budget without any consideration of what God might do. It got me thinking about being a giver in a world that has so many needs.

First, I think it's important to give what we can. Don't overextend yourself in your giving. As a college student, I've had to be picky about who and what gets what little money I have, but I am reminded of the parable Jesus tells of the widow's mite, the story in which we see that little is much in the kingdom of God.[44]

Second, I feel like we need to be careful with how we as church people or ministry partners ask for and use the money we receive. Don't make it about the church or the ministry; make it about what God can do through what is given. We are called to be good stewards of the things given to us. How can we prove that through our walking and talking? How can we be stewards and sharers of the richness of God's gifts to us?

Recently, my favorite NPR station started a pledge drive. They stated that only 6 percent of their listeners gave any money to the station. That got me thinking about churches, where some people give what they can but some don't give at all. While I certainly understand that we can't give all day, every day, God needs our resources, our time, our talents, and, yes, even our finances to continue the good work of kingdom building here on earth.

---

44. Mark 12:41-44; Luke 21:1-4.

So the next time you're asked to prayerfully consider giving, make a point to research where that money goes, learn how you might be a better steward of your resources, and, finally, be sure to give what you can when you can. For ultimately we only have so much, but that's where God comes in. God multiplies what we give for the greater good of the people here on earth. Be sure to take care of yourself and your finances when it comes time to give.

GOD AND POLITICS

NOVEMBER 7, 2014

What a week this has been in the world of politics. The dust is settling over a bitterly contested political season, and now we are left with a plethora of questions surrounding what's next and an abundance of leftover campaign signs.

Inevitably there is considerable disdain for the political world over who won and who lost. I myself found candidates whom I wanted to win who didn't win, and candidates I didn't want to win did. That's just the way politics works in our country, but I hope we can look to our response to what has happened through the lens of faith.

I once heard it said that what determines how strong we are in our faith is how we respond to the situations that disappoint us. I would add that it's also a faith indicator based on how we respond to situations that do go our way. For in the mess we call politics, I am reminded that God is neither Democrat nor Republican. To suggest anything different is a dangerous game of putting God in a box.

Different parties will take control of the White House, the House of Representatives, and the Senate, but God is a God who loves us despite our differences. There is something to be said about this world and that, even in the messiness, God is constant.

This isn't to say we shouldn't be worried about the future of our world. Quite the contrary. I saw a church here in Statesville with a sign outside that said, "Vote! Vote! Vote!" The responsibilities of freedom are bound up with our faith, and our response to the situations we face determines how we connect with God and one another.

If your party didn't win this time around, consider how you might be able to pray for the newly elected leaders despite your differences. If your party did win this time around, remind yourself that people are hurt by the loss caused by your win, so act with love and kindness despite ideological differences.

Finally, my friend Nathan Kirkpatrick said it best: "On Election Day, our children are watching. America, let's behave in a manner worthy of them." Ultimately the world and even human history watches how people of faith respond to the situations we face, whether that be politically or some other situation. So keep the faith that what you do matters, and how you react will be scrutinized.

That's why faith isn't easy; despite how inconspicuous we might like to be, people who want to see our response are always watching us. So this week, if you have something political to say, be careful how you say it because your response can reflect your faith.

Finally, always remember that God is a God of love and grace and hope. We all go vote because we all have a hope that this land will be better off for it. So pray and hope that God will work for a better life for all of us, because ultimately that's when God does God's best work.

JESUS AND THE IMMIGRANT CHILDREN

SUMMER 2014

This entire time we've been hearing about the number of children flocking to our country from Latin America,[45] I can't help but think of Jesus' words in the Gospel of Mark: "Let the little children come to me; do not stop them; for it is to such as these that the kingdom of God belongs" (10:14).

Perhaps I'm stretching things too far, but I've always believed God is among children, especially children such as these, who are working, waiting for people of faith and humanity in general to take a stand against the injustice and oppression of a broken system and situational terror. The reality is that we can no longer ignore the situation because, for better or worse, God has turned divine attention to the scene unfolding at our border.

The kingdom of God belongs to such as these. When I was in high school at the Duke Youth Academy, Dr. Stanley Hauerwas taught us about realized eschatology, that all of us play an integral role in bringing about the kingdom promised to us in the Scriptures. How is that playing out for you in this incarnation of children being tormented to a point of risking it all for safe lodging and holy rest?

What is our response as people of faith? It is simply to follow Jesus. That doesn't make the situation easier or any less complex, but in following Jesus we realize that this debate about what we should do is no debate at all. We must welcome the poor, the downtrodden, the weary souls longing to be free from oppression and despair.

---

45. Richard Cowan, "Waves of Immigrant Minors Present Crisis for Obama, Congress," Reuters.com, May 28, 2014 (reuters.com/article/us-usa-immigration-children/waves-of-immigrant-minors-present-crisis-for-obama-congress-idUSKBN0E814T20140528).

My girlfriend Stephanie is currently in France studying abroad. The other day she sent me a text saying she attended a parish church where St. Vincent De Paul celebrated mass in the seventeenth century. It brought to mind St. Vincent De Paul's own words, poignant words in the light of the situation of immigrants:

> You will find out that charity is a heavy burden to carry, heavier than the kettle of soup and the full basket. But you will keep your gentleness and your smile. It is not enough to give soup and bread. This the rich can do. You are the servant of the poor, always smiling and good-humored. They are your masters, terribly sensitive and exacting master you will see, and the uglier and the dirtier they will be, the more unjust and insulting, the more love you must give them. It is only for your love alone that the poor will forgive you the bread you give to them.[46]

Dear people of God, we must give more than bread and soup; we must give love and hope. Don't let political pride get in the way of a theological and humanitarian answer. Keep the faith that the kingdom of God belongs to the last and least of these, especially the children.

---

46. A. J. M. Mousolfe and J. K. Mousolfe, "Reflection for November 5," in *Saint Companions for Each Day* (Mumbai: St. Paul Press Training School, 1986), 417.

DIFFERENT IDEOLOGIES IN FAITH

FALL 2014

Recently, I've been hearing a lot of disagreements about different theologies, interpretations, and realities of faith. Whether it be politically charged or simply a difference of opinion, faith is something that can be fraught with tension, but it doesn't have to be.

John Wesley, the eighteenth-century theologian, was famously quoted as saying, "But as to all opinions which do not strike at the root of Christianity, we think and let think." Perhaps you're like me and try not to worry too much about what other people think. In a world where social media and other outlets allow for everyone to have their opinion publicized and commented on, no wonder there are so many facets of faith on which to disagree.

Dear readers, if you want my opinion (you're reading this, so I think you do), God revealed himself in the person of Jesus Christ as a means of grace. Even Jesus' closest companions and first apostles disagreed on issues surrounding faith. By the time we reach the end of the first century of the Common Era, we find that Peter and Paul disagreed and barely talked to one another. They found themselves at odds, but that doesn't have to be how we respond to disagreement.

We can respond to disagreement through the beauty of Christ-like love and grace. We can find ourselves disagreeing without confrontation or abrasive behavior seen all too often by Christians today. The world is a big place, and as citizens of this world we must be prepared for the reality of disagreement. That should not hinder us; it should be something that we celebrate and explore more deeply.

Think and let think. Next time you find yourself at odds with another Christian, or even with someone of a different faith or no faith at all, remember the life and teachings of Jesus, the type of person who welcomed all to the table who wanted to converse with him. Jesus didn't change their hearts with lofty theological language and combat; he changed their hearts by his love. And ultimately, friends, the world will know we are Christians by our love, not by our disagreements.

GOD'S PEACE IS IMPORTANT TO FAITH

MAY 2, 2014

I was watching *World News Tonight* when they did a piece on secondhand stress. Apparently you can catch stress. If people around you are stressed, you too might be feeling those anxieties. Though the finding about stress is fascinating, there is something to be said about trying to find a stress-free life.

Currently, I'm stressed. This is the week before finals, and I have papers due and tests looming on the horizon. I am often confronted with the stress of school, but this week seems to add an extra helping of anxiety and stress to what I normally experience. But I received news about one of my classes that helped relieve stress, and I think it had a lot to do with hard work and faith.

I'm not good at math. I may be a decent writer, but I can't for the life of me deal with equations or algebra or geometry. It's just not my cup of tea. There have been plenty of times when I have found myself working hard and wanting to give up, but a quick prayer to God for encouragement and peace helped me get through. You see, God is all about calming our fears and anxieties and stress. That's part of the economy of grace.

Now I'm confident that hard work paid off. I studied hard and worked hard to attain a passing grade in math. But honestly, I couldn't have gotten through it without the peace that passes all understanding.[47] There's something special about God working in your life to create a hope-filled and stress-reduced existence.

I'm not saying that life will always be stress-free or full of moments that are always peaceful. What I am saying is that God can work through

---

47. Phil 4:7.

situations that might seem bleak to bring us fresh reminders of God's love. There's such beauty and peace in that. God can calm the storm; no situation you're going through can keep you from God's abiding peace.

I'm reminded of the hymn that has given peace to so many: "Abide with me; fast falls the eventide; the darkness deepens; Lord with me abide. When other helpers fail and comforts flee, Help of the helpless, O abide with me."[48]

Friends, be confident in the beauty of the help of the helpless. Be confident that you can be a part of God's peace, and pass that peace on to others who might need it. To borrow and slightly edit a quote from Gandhi, be the peace you want to see in the world. That way, God can work through you and you can be a small miracle for countless others. Be at peace, and let the Lord abide with you.

---

48. Henry Francis Lyte, "Abide with Me" (1847).

THANKING GOD FOR SECOND CHANCES

MAY 30, 2014

Maya Angelou, the poet genius of our time and civil rights activist, died this week. She inspired me in so many ways; she inspired so many in ways that will become apparent as time marches forward. I wanted to share my favorite quote attributed to her and possibly connect it to our lives in faith.

> I've learned that no matter what happens, or how bad it seems today, life does go on, and it will be better tomorrow. I've learned that you can tell a lot about a person by the way he/she handles these three things: a rainy day, lost luggage, and tangled Christmas tree lights. I've learned that regardless of your relationship with your parents, you'll miss them when they're gone from your life. I've learned that making a "living" is not the same thing as making a "life." I've learned that life sometimes gives you a second chance. I've learned that you shouldn't go through life with a catcher's mitt on both hands; you need to be able to throw something back. I've learned that whenever I decide something with an open heart, I usually make the right decision. I've learned that even when I have pains, I don't have to be one. I've learned that every day you should reach out and touch someone. People love a warm hug, or just a friendly pat on the back. I've learned that I still have a lot to learn. I've learned that people will forget what you said, people will forget what you did, but people will never forget how you made them feel.[49]

---

49. From an interview on *Oprah*, aired April 4, 2002.

Friends, how do you handle tangled Christmas tree lights? How has God worked in your life to give you second chances? You see, this life we live is part of the beautiful reality God is working to restore in our broken lives. This week, hug someone, reach out to someone, and remember that you still have a lot to learn.

Most important, make a difference in this world. Make a difference in this world for God. Make a difference in this world for grace, love, and hope. I saw the new X-Men movie, and in it, Professor Xavier describes hope as the most basic human emotion, but in it there is such power and strength. Hope for a brighter tomorrow, as Maya Angelou did. Work to make that tomorrow happen, and you never know what you might accomplish. Thanks be to God for Maya Angelou, and thanks be to God for what God is working to accomplish in our lives.

Rest in peace, dear soul.

GROUNDED IN FAITH AND SCRIPTURE

> *That it is precisely when we recognize our common humanity—when we recognize our own humanity in the face of the other—it is then that we also recognize the face of God.*
> —Diana Butler Bass in Grounded

Even though I served as a newspaper columnist and wrote primarily for that purpose for some time, I am a pastor first. I believe that I can convey my faith without being presumptuous through my pen. So I wrote for accessibility and compassion, and these articles convey that best.

STAY GROUNDED IN FAITH

NOVEMBER 16, 2017

The other day I went fly-fishing with a clergy colleague, Vern Collins, and a bishop with a reputation, Will Willimon. We went down to Boone Fork River to fish the waters surrounding Watauga County and found ourselves lost to the outside world. There was very little phone signal or connection to the realities outside of our conversations. But one conversation caught me off guard and made me think about our lives of faith.

"What do you do to keep yourself grounded?" Vern asked me, meaning no real harm in the question. I asked him what he meant. He said something along the lines that fishing and other outdoor activities made him feel connected to the world and to God.

I wish I could have had an answer for him. I said I loved "just hanging out," but I know deep down that wasn't the real answer. Will knew it and looked at me. Later on that day, the good bishop said that in all of the fray I needed to find that thing and those people who ground me to the point of keeping me sane in the midst of this thing called life.

I don't know if that's hard for you, but that's incredibly hard for me. I have a tendency to say "yes" to everything and try to be everything for everybody. I forget to ground myself in the people and things (yes, even poodles) that mean the most to me. We can't get through this life alone.

We simply and directly are not meant to be loners on the journey toward wholeness. Perhaps this week you could join me in working toward finding those things that connect you to the community. Whether it is at worship or your place of work or while you're on holiday vacation, stay grounded in the God who has created you and the Spirit who continues to sustain you.

I will never forget that day on the river when Vern and Will called my bluff on what keeps me grounded. We caught four beautiful fish that day. But also it has the potential to be a turning point to where I can spend more quality time with loved ones and activities that bring me to the heart of God. That is a mission worth acting on. Let's do this together. I hope you'll join me in being grounded in faith and hope, in love and charity toward others and ourselves.

WORSHIPING DURING THE WEEK

MAY 3, 2013

I want to tell you about my friend Ethan. I met Ethan at the church I serve. Ethan is a man about town; everyone knows when Ethan is around, and he makes sure of it. This strapping young two-year-old is the epitome of rambunctious mischief around the church and in our community, and I adore him. He'll always come to the church office to visit, and he'll come find me to tell the most wonderful stories about his adventures for the day. This past week, I got to have lunch with him, and I felt incredibly close to the heart of God.

We went to a local restaurant in town, and Ethan was so excited to get to eat some good food and hang out with his family. He was sure to share his chips and salsa with us, making it easy on all those gathered round him by dipping the chip in the salsa and then handing it to each of us in the order of our seats around the booth. When the food came, somberness crawled across his face; he was sure that this was a serious moment. His dad asked him to say the blessing, and he knew this was his time to shine.

If you've ever heard a two-year-old pray, I'm pretty sure you've seen a glimpse of the kingdom of God. This unintelligible prayer was later translated by his parents as best they could. "Thank you, God, for my food, for Mom's food, for Dad's food, for Rob's food, and for the chips. Amen." This was not an eloquent recitation of prayer that we've all become accustomed to in Sunday worship. This was an earnest and fervent prayer of thanksgiving. I couldn't have been more awe-inspired in that moment.

Our daily lives—not just Sunday mornings—are filled with moments of worship. For me that day, my minister was a two-year-old feeding us with spiritual food of prayer and passing out a Eucharistic feast of chips and salsa. We were in communion in one of the holiest moments of my week.

We forsake these moments, don't we? We commit them to memory because they didn't happen in the conventional way we were comfortable grasping or understanding.

God, in such magnificent love, extends to us these worship-filled weekday moments to keep us going. We come together as a community on Sunday and worship, which is important. But those moments when we feel close to the heart of God during the week are remarkably full of grace, hope, and peace. Enjoy them, embrace them, and worship through them. Because God is there in the prayers of a two-year-old and in communion around a table, weaving the presence of the Divine within our daily lives. This week, find those moments and cling to them, for they are evidence of the very heart of God.

LEARNING TO WALK ON WATER

SUMMER 2013

I once saw a saying that really spoke to me: "Be like Jesus; rebuke the storm, and if it persists, walk on it." How many times have storms taken control of our lives? How many times have we forgotten that the Master of all storms is on our side? We forsake the God of the storm for the fear that something might happen to us during that storm.

A special person in my life loves dancing in thunderstorms. One thing you must realize about me is that I tend to be a lot older than I actually am, so this concept of dancing in the rain is foreign to me. Storms are something that inspire fear; the fierce force of nature often seems to be a paradox of dancing. I am reminded of the hymn that was written in the 1960s and had these words:

> I danced on a Friday when the sky turned black
> it's hard to dance with the devil on your back.
> They buried my body and they thought I'd gone,
> but I am the Dance and I still go on![50]

Friends, living this life is an art. My dog Rusty is terrified of thunderstorms. One of the things I have to do for him is cradle him when the thunder comes. There are people in your life whom you will need when the thunder comes. People who will cradle you, people who will tell you that the storm will pass. People of faith, cherish those special individuals,

---

50. Sydney Carter, "Lord of the Dance" (Carol Stream, IL: Hope Publishing Co., 1963).

for they are the very light of life that is present for us. Small incarnate gifts of grace.

I might try dancing in the rain the next time a storm comes. Life is all about learning that Jesus walked above the toiling sea. Life is all about knowing that Jesus Christ became human so that we might experience the reality of love in this life, even amid the storm.

The last stanza of the hymn I mentioned earlier goes like this:

> They cut me down and I leapt up high,
>   I am the Life that'll never, never die;
> I'll live in you if you'll live in me;
>   I am the Lord of the Dance, said he.

Friends dance wherever you are in life. Dance in the midst of death, dance in the midst of sickness and health. Dance in the midst of toil and trouble, dance in the midst of joy and triumph. To go back to the hymn's chorus, "Dance, then, wherever you may be, I am the Lord of the Dance, said he." Simply and directly put, when all has been said and all has been done, life is about learning to dance in the rain.

USE YOUR TIME WISELY

SUMMER 2013

There's a great line in the movie *Star Trek: Generations* where the antagonist quotes mid-century poet Delmore Schwartz: "Time is the fire in which we all burn." Have you ever felt like you were running out of time?

I've spent the past two weeks moving boxes and furniture into my new apartment in Durham. My calendar is filling up with obligations at Duke, and frankly it feels like I never have enough time. But then I'm reminded of another quote from the book *My Bright Abyss: Meditation of a Modern Believer*, where Christian Wiman writes, "The greatest mistake we make is not living in time, in both senses of the phrase."

Time is a fickle friend; it is one part of our being of which we have limited resources. Yet God calls us to live in time and space; we are creatures of time. So how do we make the most of the time we have? We take the time to linger a while at the dinner table, put the phone away during a conversation, or sit with a dying loved one for a few more minutes before returning to the realities of everyday life. People on their deathbeds don't say, "Gosh, I wish I would have worked more hours" or "I wish I would've made more money." The reality is that people wish they had more time.

This week, celebrate what God has given you, especially your most precious asset: your time. God will do a good work in the time you have and create a space for grace to be present. Be present in the moment and remember whose you are. For in time we find that God entered into human history in the person of Jesus Christ. We know that God became incarnate in time for the sake of the human story. So enjoy time and find it meaningful. We are creatures of time, and may we be wise enough to use it well.

DON'T LET PEOPLE ROB YOU OF YOUR JOY

JANUARY 2012

Recently, I attended a late-night worship service at Clark's Chapel Baptist Church on Eufola Road here in Statesville. Pastor Charles Mingo was welcoming and gracious in making sure I was comfortable during the service; it was a truly wonderful experience. This service commemorated the passing of 2011 and the beginning of 2012. As the service progressed, the time came for a testimony from some in the congregation. A lady stood up for the testimony, a lady I had come to know, like much of the church had, as Mother Aleen.

Now Mother Aleen was speaking of the past year, and she said something so incredibly profound that I was taken aback at the significance of this in our daily lives. She proclaimed, "Don't let people rob you of your joy. God gave you that joy; don't let others take that away." We live in a world in which joy is hard to come by. If you look around you, you see politicians squabbling over the hot topic of the day, you see wars across the planet that threaten global stability, you see people who can't eat meals to keep themselves alive. How can we be joyful amid the sorrow and pain?

That night I realized that joy is something beyond the measure of human capability. We'd rather crucify joy than find hope in it. We are toiling in our own pain and God injects our lives with a new and gracious joy. God comes and tears open our sorrow with joy. What hope? What peace? As the old hymn goes, "Joyful, joyful, we adore Thee, God of glory, Lord of love; Hearts unfold like flowers before Thee, opening to the sun above. Melt the clouds of sin and sadness; drive the dark of doubt away; Giver of immortal gladness, fill us with the light of day!"[51] As we are filled

---

51. Henry Van Dyke, "Joyful, Joyful, We Adore Thee" (1907).

with the light of day, we see the grace of our Savior as part of our own lives. God is love, but in that love we also see the joy of grace and peace. So as our world sometimes crumbles around us, simply ask for joy, and, by God, don't let anybody steal that joy from you.

I once heard the phrase, "God is dying to meet you." While I ponder that statement from the perspective of a mainline faith, I see this, "God is dying to show you joy." This time of year, we forget the joy that comes after the cross because we're too busy still wrapped up in the beginning of the year. We are tempted to forget about the death of Jesus; we are tempted to forget the pain of the world. Theologian Stanley Hauerwas puts it this way: "It's all about love and joy. The light has come into the world, but the light that illuminates from the cross does not rid the world of snakes trying to get at you." Dr. Hauerwas goes on to say, "To be raised with Christ means the end of any attempt to passively stare and sometimes forget about the crucifixion. You cannot stare at that in which you participate."

Thanks be to God that we die and are raised in joy with Christ. By all means, protect that joy.

FIND SACRED SPACES AND RELATIONSHIPS

AUGUST 2012

I have so many wonderful friends and family, and this week I've been spending time with them in Boone and Statesville for my spring reading week. I've been catching up over coffee at my favorite coffee shop, Espresso News; I've been eating my favorite chili at Boone Saloon; and I've been spending time with my mom and dad at my home on St. Cloud Drive.

I tell you this because this Lenten season, I've been contemplating the idea of thin places. The Celtic people had this incredible idea that there are places in this world in which you can reach out and touch the center and ground of being. You can be so close to the God of time and space that you can feel it in your bones.

All these places I mentioned above are thin places for me. They are not thin places because of their geographical location (though the air is thin in Boone, for sure). They are thin because of the people who inhabit those spaces with me. Time stands still in Espresso News when conversations begin. Life seems sweeter when the chili is served while I'm sitting next to a close friend or loved one. It all makes sense when I'm at home on St. Cloud Drive.

I'm starting to think we're not supposed to have it all figured out. I know at twenty-four, I know less now than I did six years ago at eighteen. But isn't that kind of the point? Being lost in the great unknown and finding God there is the point of our existence. For God did not come to provide certainty but instead to provide an encounter with a stranger on the road or a friend at a coffee shop.

Mary Oliver has become one of my favorite poets over the years, and part of her poem "Roses" goes like this:

Everyone now and again wonders about
those questions that have no ready
answers . . .

"Wild roses," I said to them one morning.
"Do you have the answers? And if you do,
would you tell me?"

The roses laughed softly. "Forgive us,"
they said. "But as you can see, we are
just now entirely busy being roses."[52]

If we live like the roses, totally consumed by the beauty of friendship and fellowship, Lent might seem a little less desolate. Lent is that time where we mark the beauty of what Christ did for us in the waning moments of his ministry and life. But then, off in the distance, the roses begin to bloom again and resurrection is just around the bend.

My challenge to you this week is simple: find the thin places in the sacred relationships and places you have. Whether that is at Broad Street Burger, Wine Maestro, or your childhood home down on your road, may you see more clearly that you belong to God. Because God is found and defined in love. Blessings this Lenten season.

---

52. "Roses," in *Felicity* (New York: Penguin Books, 2017), 7.

READING SCRIPTURE IS IMPORTANT TO OUR FAITH

JULY 4, 2014

Currently, I'm doing an independent study with one of my professors at Appalachian [State University]. We're talking about Ecclesiastes, a book of wisdom in the Hebrew Bible. Part of my assignment is to pore over the text using commentaries and guides to help me better understand what the writer of Ecclesiastes is trying to say. That got me thinking about our faith.

When was the last time we pored over a book of Scripture trying to understand or contextualize what the author was saying? When was the last time we had a conversation with someone where we tried the art of interpreting what a biblical author was trying to articulate in the message of the book? If you're anything like me, sometimes our busy lives get in the way of reading Scripture or commentary on Scripture. Too many times we're going places or watching our favorite television show or just plain don't have any energy left to read Scripture, but it is so important to our faith.

The books of the Old and New Testament contain valuable insight on how to live life, on how to structure our faith and remind us of the value of our souls. There is such hope in the reality that we have books that can guide us in the way of life, but I must warn you as well: there can be a danger in worshiping the Bible instead of the God who inspired the Bible.

Let me explain: Every time we open the Scriptures, we bring with it our own selves. We read it based on our context as twenty-first-century Americans of a certain race or ethnic group and countless other means of context. In doing so we have the potential to bring our own baggage to the Scriptures and interpret it in a way that is dangerous. Take for example the interpretations that slavery was okay during the 1800s due to a certain reading of Scripture. We must always be careful to look at the Bible for what it is and continue to seek God's inspiration in its words.

This week I challenge you to read a book of the Bible you haven't read before. If you're looking for a good New Testament one, try James. If you're more in the mood for something out of the Hebrew Bible, try Malachi or Micah. Keep in mind what you bring to the text and read carefully. Try to find what God is saying—you never know what might be in store.

DISAPPOINTMENTS FUEL OUR FAITH

SEPTEMBER 19, 2014

Let's be honest with one another. I have problems with writing sometimes. As much as I enjoy writing to you all every week, sometimes it becomes a daunting task. A lot of times I'll be disappointed in myself or my week because I honestly don't have much to say. I remember someone telling me that the difference between a good writer and a great writer is that the great writers write, even when they don't want to.

Have you ever been disappointed in yourself or your situation? Have you ever been so lost that the reality of your life doesn't make coherent sense or your sanity is in question because of all that has happened? I think I know the answer to that question, but I'm also reminded that's where God comes in.

God takes our disappointments and allows them to fuel our faith. The bright hope of tomorrow is reminiscent of what the psalmist said when they wrote, "Sorrow may last for the night, but joy comes in the morning."[53]

Our lives are lived between joy and sorrow; the scales of our lives are weighed between the two, but I'm reminded of a card I saw the other day that said, "Leave yesterday behind. Let hope guide you to a sunny new tomorrow."

Let God take your disappointments and restore you to resurrection. Let God take the hope of the future and breathe the life of that reality into your dry bones. I often think of the hymn "Great Is Thy Faithfulness." It has lyrics such as these: "Pardon for sin and a peace that endureth, thine own dear presence to cheer and to guide; Strength for today and bright hope for tomorrow, blessing all mine, with ten thousand beside! Great is

---

53. Ps 30:5.

thy faithfulness! Great is thy faithfulness! Morning by morning new mercies I see. All I have needed thy hand hath provided. Great is thy faithfulness, Lord, unto me!"[54]

Keep the faith, dear friends. Don't let disappointment in yourself consume you or dictate your future. This can be lived out in concrete ways—you can finally go back to college, you can finally take a leap of faith and leave your current job for something new and wonderful on the horizon, you can get back to church even though it's been way too long. In all those situations and countless more, God is present to take any disappointment we might have in ourselves and turn it into a leap of faith. Strength for today, bright hope for tomorrow: God is blessing you in countless ways. So take that leap of faith and let God love you into tomorrow.

Back to what I first told you about a good writer and a great writer, let me offer a different version of that statement. The difference between good people of faith and great people of faith is that the great people of faith keep singing in the darkness, even when they don't want to. All I have needed thy hand hath provided; great is thy faithfulness, Lord, unto me!

---

54. Thomas O. Chisholm, "Great Is Thy Faithfulness, O God My Father" (1923).

THE EFFORT TO LIVE A LIFE WORTHY OF FAITH

SUMMER 2015

With some upcoming scholarship interviews and other meetings to help prepare for the next three years at Duke Divinity School, I've pondered a piece of Scripture that has become a favorite of mine these past few months.

In the book of Ephesians, Paul writes to the church of Ephesus in the fourth chapter, "I therefore, a prisoner in the Lord, beg you to lead a life worthy of the calling to which you have been called." The book of Colossians echoes this in the first chapter when it says, ". . . so that you may lead lives worthy of the Lord, fully pleasing to him, as you bear fruit in every good work and as you grow in the knowledge of God."

Living a worthy life. Some Christians might argue that it isn't possible to do. I would tend to disagree with them. I think that we are all, as John Wesley said, "moving on to perfection." We're all working toward living a life worthy of the gospel, worthy of our calling. We're not guaranteed success; in fact, I'd say that we're guaranteed failure. We will never 100 percent fully live into the calling God has for us, but that doesn't mean we can't try.

What does that look like for you? Perhaps it means taking a leap of faith or knowing when to stop what you're doing for something new. Maybe it's reading more Scripture or praying more often. Whatever the case, be sure to take the steps so that you are living into the calling God has placed on your life.

Brothers and sisters, we are called to be human. Yes, that sounds a little weird, but I fully believe that God has called us to be fully human. That means we can't do everything for everyone, we can't be everywhere all the time, and that's part of living into our calling. We must give everything over to God, do our best, and allow things to work out the way God has planned.

Don't ever give up on your calling. Let it sustain you and nurture you; let it challenge you and wrestle with you. For our callings from God are the closest link we have to God in Christ Jesus. Hear the good news, friends: We are called. We are chosen and favored people. Keep the faith that your calling is important, and live into your calling more fully each passing day.

THE ART OF LISTENING

FALL 2014

One of my favorite stories in all of Scripture is from 1 Kings:

> [The voice of God] said, "Go out and stand on the mountain before the LORD, for the LORD is about to pass by." Now there was a great wind, so strong that it was splitting mountains and breaking rocks in pieces before the LORD, but the LORD was not in the wind; and after the wind an earthquake, but the LORD was not in the earthquake; and after the earthquake a fire, the LORD was not in the fire; and after the fire a sound of sheer silence. When Elijah heard it, he wrapped his face in his mantle and went out and stood at the entrance of the cave. Then there came a voice to him that said, "What are you doing here, Elijah?" (1 Kgs 19:11-13)

The beauty of the story is that Elijah had to listen for God's still, small voice in the silence. God was present in a way that Elijah probably least expected God to be. Have you ever had trouble listening? I know I have; people talking to us are often met with deaf ears as we are busy planning our day, looking at our phones, or making grocery lists in our heads. Perhaps we can look at listening as an act of faith.

God doesn't have to come in the bright and flashy lights of faith; in fact, sometimes God doesn't intend to come that way precisely because God wants to reach us with a still, small voice. Our job is to be open to this beautiful message God has to share with us.

Last week I was listening to an NPR special on listening and how we have to breathe and take time to really hear what other people are saying to us if we want to live a genuine life. I think that's important for us to hear as we spend our days listening to others and to God. Try listening this week; you never know what you might hear.

LISTENING IS AN ACT OF FAITH

JUNE 27, 2014

Recently during my summer school classes, I've had to participate in listening journals. For these listening journals, we have to listen to a piece of music and then review what we've heard. To listen to a piece of music may sound easy, but for these journals I've really had to concentrate on the musicality, tone, and texture of the music. This got me thinking about listening and how it can be an act of faith.

Do you ever listen to someone and not really hear what they're saying? There is a tendency in our culture to be on our phones, on our computers, or have other distractions in the way of our listening. There is such danger in that because ultimately people need to be heard.

I can remember when I first came to the church I serve and someone walked into my office and told me a painful story. I didn't say anything, but I sat in silence for a few minutes pondering the story that was just given to me. After a moment, the person stood up and walked out of the room, saying all she had needed was for someone to listen to her story.

God, in God's infinite wisdom, gave us people to surround us and listen to us. Listening can be an act of faith because it can be a way of healing what someone is going through and support and surround that person in an incarnational fashion.

This week, be God's listening ear to someone in need. Put down the cell phone and genuinely hear what people are saying. Put away the grocery list and listen to the joys and sorrows of going through this life we live. It's a glorious existence, but it needs to be shared.

GOD CREATED THE SABBATH FOR A REASON: FINDING PEACE

MARCH 7, 2014

Appalachian State University's spring break is next week, and I couldn't be more thrilled. It has been a long semester full of work and classes. While I enjoyed the challenge, I found myself yearning for this break more than ever. It's been a hard winter here in the mountains of North Carolina, and I'm ready to spend an extended period of time with family and friends at home in Statesville.

That got me thinking about our lives of faith. We all need rest as human beings, but our souls need rest as well. We go through our weeks with the hustle of daily work and often forget the importance of rest. I once heard it said that we need to take time to rest because often our souls have to catch up with our bodies.

How does this play out for you in your life? Are you at a place where you are able to take Sabbath rest? I'm not just talking about going to church on Sunday (though that can be a part of Sabbath rest and rejuvenation); I'm talking about the deep inner peace of finding yourself resting in God's grace and love.

We've begun the season of Lent in the life of the church, and we hear about people giving something up for this season. Perhaps you could take on the spiritual discipline of Sabbath rest along with giving something up. Habits can be hard to form, but God calls us to be a part of the rest God instated for us when he rested on the seventh day.

How are you going to find that peace? We all so desperately need to sit with the quietness of our own souls and the quietness of God. I am reminded of the story of Elijah and how he found God not in the wind or the fire or the earthquake but in the still, small voice. Listen for that still, small voice; find it in your own life. You must cherish the ability to rest.

As I write this, I'm watching my dog nap near me. It reminds me that the whole of creation needs to rest, and we are not immune from that. Sometimes we just need to remind ourselves that God's love for us is a love that wants what's best for us. Look for that this week, and find consolation in the Sabbath God gives us.

SMALL-TOWN CONSTRUCTION

SPRING 2015

When people ask me to describe where I'm from, I often say that when you get to where Interstate 40 and 77 meet, there's Statesville. I'm sure you've all seen the construction going on there, the re-mapping of the roads we have known for decades. We've also heard a lot of coverage over the proposed Love's Truck Stop. A professor the other day here at Appalachian mentioned to me that he heard Statesville was having what we in the South call a "heated discussion" over the pros and cons of building that truck stop. I'll spare you the details of how I feel about all this construction and let you know how I see it from a faith perspective.

We're all a little like Statesville. We all are caught between growth and what we know to be our identity. I think that during all of our lives we have little (and sometimes not so little) construction projects going on in the landscape of our reality. On the converse side of that, we often have demolition projects going on. We aren't the same people we were five years ago; our existence is a little different than what it will be ten years from now. This may cause alarm to some, but in the beauty of faith it is a good thing.

I'm pretty sure God is the best construction manager I've ever encountered. Since the dawn of our existence as the human race and our own personal lives, God has been weaving God's way throughout time and space to make known God's love for us. This may come in construction projects, through help for an addition, in the marriage, or through the friendship. It may come in demolition projects as you learn to let go of your tattered past and celebrate God's future. It may come as you realize that your friends weren't the healthiest for you. All these beautiful reminders of love articulate God's abounding hope spread throughout everything we hold dear.

So this week, be thankful that there are construction projects going on in our community and in our lives. Because for us to be stagnant, or never changing, is to forget the life God calls us to. That isn't to say that you should never be still and hear the still, small voice in the silence. It is to note that we all go at different speeds at different times in our lives, and that is a beautiful reminder of our commonality that is tied to our Creator.

I'm not the person I was a year ago, and though that is a normal part of the life cycle that could easily cause pain, bitterness, and resentment, I praise God in the knowledge that God isn't done with me or us yet. There's still work to be done. There's still more to be built.

GOD'S ANSWER TO ANXIETY IS FAITH

FEBRUARY 14, 2014

I don't know about you, but all this winter weather has left me anxious. Anxious for the road workers and people who have to brave the weather, anxious as to whether I have enough milk and bread in case I get snowed in, and the list goes on. It got me thinking about our lives of faith and how we are anxious in every part of our lives.

We walk through this life with certain anxieties; that's part of the human condition. But God's answer to our anxiety is faith. God reminds us of this in the Scriptures when Paul says in his letter to the Philippians, "Do not be anxious about anything, but in every situation, by prayer and petition, with thanksgiving, present your requests to God. And the peace of God, which transcends all understanding, will guard your hearts and your minds in Christ Jesus" (Phil 4:6-7).

In every situation, God's peace surrounds us and guards us. What comfort is that? What joy does it bring the soul to know that God is with us in our most anxious moments? So when the winter storms of life bear down on us, let us be reminded of God's abiding presence in our lives. As the snow falls, I am reminded of the old standard of church hymnody: "Through many dangers, toils and snares, I have already come; 'Tis grace hath brought me safe thus far, And grace will lead me home. The Lord has promised good to me, His Word my hope secures; He will my Shield and Portion be, As long as life endures."[55]

When life seems at its worst because of anxiety or the storms of life, be reminded that God is working to bring you out of the storm. God is at work to bring to fruition the love first made evident in Jesus Christ. God

---

55. John Newton, "Amazing Grace" (1779).

has already won against our anxieties, God has already won against the storm, against the pain, the heartache, and the realities that seek to bind us and keep us down.

So this week, as the storms rage and life seems bad, remember that God is the best presence we have in our lives. God is the best reality we could ever hope for, and, more important, God's love is real and we have an eternal hope in that. That's the most incredible reality we could ever hope for. Be thankful for that in your life.

GOD CARES ABOUT YOUR SOUL

FEBRUARY 21, 2014

Have you ever heard the story of the old hymn, "It Is Well with My Soul"? I was reminded this week of why the hymnist Horatio Spafford wrote the hymn in the late 1800s.

Spafford's life was in ruins. The 1871 Great Chicago Fire destroyed his business, and his life was devastated in 1873 when he sent his family ahead of him on a trip to Europe on the *SS Ville du Havre*. The ship sank and all four of his children died. His wife Anna was the only person in his family who survived the sinking.

Spafford later wrote the famous hymn to commemorate his daughters: "When peace, like a river, attendeth my way, when sorrows like sea billows roll; whatever my lot, thou hast taught me to say, it is well, it is well, with my soul."

What consolation to know that God cares for our souls! The God who created us does not leave us stranded as we face life's most daunting moments. The God who loves us gives us peace like a river so that we too can find ourselves lost in the grace of the Divine.

Friends, I don't know about you, but that gets me through this life. To know and to share the life-changing grace of Jesus Christ is to experience such peace when life is at its worst. Even when you're down on your luck, you have the potential to share your story. We have the promise of grace and the hope of the resurrection throughout our lives.

This week, I challenge you to remember that God's love and peace are a part of the economy of grace. God cares about your soul. God cares about your well-being. This isn't to say that things will always be good for you or that all will be right in your world. It means that God spends all of our lives spinning redemptive grace into the fabric of our being.

Keep the faith, for God is at work. Know that there is more to life than the trials we face. When things are at their worst, remember Spafford and his hymn that reminds us that it is well with our souls. God is for us, and if God is for us, what possibly could be against us?

IN REMEMBRANCE, THERE IS LIFE

MAY 23, 2014

This weekend, the church I serve will celebrate the college and high school graduates who have accomplished so much this year. Part of the challenge I will deliver to them is to "prayerfully remember what God has done in your life and joyously look forward to all that God has in store for you." That's a good way to look at things, especially on Memorial Day weekend.

Memorial Day's history can be traced as far back as the Civil War when soldiers' graves were decorated in the month of May. This is a somber time for many Americans who commemorate the loss of people giving the ultimate sacrifice for the country they love. It made me think of a well-known passage in the New Testament, and I hope we can all learn from it.

John 15 has words such as these: "This is my commandment, that you love one another as I have loved you. No one has greater love than this, than to lay down one's life for one's friends" (vv. 12-13). Christ gave the ultimate sacrifice in all of human history. We threw death at Christ and Christ gave us Easter morning. There is such hope and such peace in knowing that Christ laughed at death and found new resurrection in the face of a tomb.

We all will have our own Easter morning; that's why we can joyously look forward to all that God has in store for us. Keep the faith that God is working to create an Easter of unending joy in your life as well.

Some of you may be thinking that Easter was a month ago and we should be moving on by now. The church, however, views Easter as fifty days between Easter Sunday and Pentecost. We are called to remember and memorialize Easter for as long as we live.

I have a sheet of cloth from the Holocaust Museum in Washington, DC, that states, "In remembrance, there is life." Friends, this Memorial Day, remember Easter; remember the resurrection that can happen for us.

Remember that in our memories there is life, and know that our futures are filled with hope. Thanks be to God for remembering us!

YOUR FAITH LETTER OF REFERENCE

FEBRUARY 9, 2017

I've been applying to PhD programs and jobs over the course of the past few weeks as I prepare to graduate from Duke. I've been having to go around to professors, clergy, and former parishioners asking for letters of reference for these programs and jobs. It's a really interesting reality in the theological world because often the programs and jobs have asked the writers of my letters of reference to comment on my faith and capacity for theological thought. So let me pose the question to you: if you asked the people around you for a letter of reference about your faith, what might people say?

Would people surrounding you say you wear your faith on your sleeve, or are you more reserved? Do you speak up and speak out, or do you keep a calm reserve of faith that gets you through the day? Whatever the case, I'm curious what people would think of your faith. Now don't hear me wrong; for many, religion and faith are personal. But still, I am reminded that we are known by our fruits. So how are your fruits faring these days?

If anything, we must be known by how we interact with others. I'm not suggesting that you leave everything behind and enter a life of vocational ministry. But as the adage goes, "Preach the gospel; use words if necessary." May we be emboldened to have strong letters of reference for our faith. I love the hymn with the words, "They will know we are Christians by our love." May we have strong letters of reference because we are known for love and not judgment, hope and not despair, grace and not condemnation. It is in this mindset that the faithful will flourish and the church will continue to be vibrant.

Look for strong letters of faith reference, and may your faith represent who you are and whose you are. May God richly bless you this week, so that you in turn may bless others.

CHALLENGES ARE PART OF LIFE

JANUARY 31, 2014

During the winter, the wind and the cold can often get to people. Living in the Appalachian Mountains, I have to deal with plenty of wind and snow. The challenges of getting to class can be daunting; often I have to face into the wind and snow to get to my desired location on campus.

Have you ever had to face a challenge that seems daunting? Have you ever had to face into something that you'd much rather skip and not deal with? We all have those situations in life that challenge us to our very core. What are we to do with those situations? How are we to face into the winds, rain, and snowstorms of life?

Luckily, God faces into those storms with us. God doesn't shield us from the challenges of life—that wouldn't be fruitful. Instead, God works through the storms of life to keep us in the palm of God's hand. Whatever you are facing, however you are facing it, God is calling to you through the wind, the rain, and the snow. God is calling us to be a resilient people but not to worry because God gives us the tools necessary to face our challenges.

Or think of it this way: one of the things we all know is that the nights of winter can be the hardest and coldest to face. Here in Boone, the wind chill has been minus 15 degrees at times. We too face those long cold nights of our lives; however, I am reminded of what the psalmist said: "His favor is for a lifetime. Weeping may linger for the night, but joy comes with the morning" (Ps 30:5).

This week, as winter storms surround us, be reminded of the grace of God. Find solace and warmth in the reality that God is with us and God is for God's people. We can face whatever we have on the horizon with dignity and hope because God is present and love is here.

Find peace in God's abiding presence. Don't fear the storms of life, because God is accomplishing a good work in you and finding a way to bring you through the storm. I am reminded that Jesus never said it would be easy; he said that we would never be alone. We would have an advocate and a friend in the one who creates and sustains us. Just remember that old gospel standard: "What a friend we have in Jesus, all our sins and griefs to bear! What a privilege to carry everything to God in prayer! O what peace we often forfeit, O what needless pain we bear. All because we do not carry everything to God in prayer."[56]

Go into the world this week knowing that God goes with you to walk beside you, to comfort and strengthen you. But more important, God gives us the deep, deep peace that allows us to face into whatever lies in store.

---

56. Joseph Medlicott Scriven, "What a Friend We Have in Jesus" (1855).

FAITH IS A LESSON IN SLOWING DOWN, LEARNING TO READ AGAIN

JANUARY 10, 2014

I have always loved to read. I can remember the late nights reading the next great novel put out by the proverbial children's writers of the late 1990s. I still love to read, but I've gotten into a horrible habit: I look ahead to see when the chapter I'm reading ends so I can figure out how long I have to get to the next chapter, the next section, the next resting space in which I can choose to put the book down or keep reading late into the night.

We're so busy and rushed. Perhaps it's because we've gotten tired. We have sleepless nights because of illness, money, pain, or any possible suffering imaginable. That got me thinking about a little psalm that is attributed to David when he was captured by the Philistines—Psalm 56. Eugene H. Peterson's Bible translation *The Message* puts verse 8 this way: "You've kept track of my every toss and turn through the sleepless nights, each tear entered in your ledger, each ache written in your book."

If we can take God at God's promise, then God can certainly teach us to read again. There are constant examples of this in our lives where God is rewriting our chapter: to fall in love so deeply that the next chapter doesn't matter, to be lost in such a beautiful sunset that our worries and cares don't require the next chapter, to have family and friends surrounding us in sorrow and in joy. When we let God rewrite our chapter, we will have learned to read again. That's what we all need—the ability to slow down and not search for the next chapter—because eventually there won't be any chapters left and we all will turn and sigh at the moments we could have enjoyed and cherished.

As the psalmist proclaims, God's enveloping grace puts an end to things that we suffer from in this transient life. The renewing hope of everything we know about the divine promises to us is that, though there are moments when we curse the very thought of God, the awe-inspiring creator continues to hold the tears, the pain, the mental illnesses, the physical illnesses, the suffering, and the grief in his love.

So learn to read again. Learn to look at this very moment as an opportunity to make a memory to remember for your time on earth. Challenge yourself anew to face tomorrow with grace and dignity, for God is on your side. Learn to read not chapter to chapter but in a wonderful odyssey through life. If you've ever read a good book, you'll know that the chapters don't matter as much because you're lost in the book. In the same way, with life you have the potential to be "lost in wonder, love, and praise" as Charles Wesley penned.[57] We are bound for bigger things than chapters, so start reading your book again.

---

57. "Love Divine, All Loves Excelling" (1747).

SERMONS OF PUBLIC THEOLOGY

Cheap grace is the deadly enemy of our church. We are fighting today for costly grace.
—Dietrich Bonhoeffer *(from* The Cost of Discipleship*)*

This chapter contains three sermons that have influenced my writing, my preaching, everything—they truly have made me what I am. The first one is from Harvard's Memorial Church where I preached at a storied pulpit after leaving my own pulpit a year prior. The second is a sermon from the Historic Ebenezer Baptist Church, the church of the Rev. Dr. Martin Luther King Jr. The experience was a dream of his realized as the sons of former slaves and the sons of former slave owners joined hands. The third is a sermon I preached at Maranatha Baptist Church where Jimmy Carter attends and teaches Sunday school. My wife Stephanie even got to cook lasagna for the former President and First Lady while we were there. It's a memory we will forever cherish.

HARVARD UNIVERSITY'S MEMORIAL CHURCH

FEBRUARY 18, 2018

To Professor Walton and the clergy of Harvard's Memorial Church: I am blessed because this is a dream come true. Thank you for your hospitality and invitation.

Won't you pray with me?

May the words of my mouth and the meditations of all our hearts be acceptable in your sight, for you and you alone are our strong rock and our redeemer. Amen.

This past week, my little brother Scott, a senior at the University of North Carolina School of the Arts, a conservatory in my home state, performed in an opera from a story we have all heard before. However, in this particular instance I saw the story with new eyes because of Scott. The AJ Fletcher Opera Institute performed Rossini's *Cinderella*—the old, old story of a woman transfigured from ashes to the beauty and splendor of the kingdom. This story came alive for me in new ways because my younger brother offered to us a deep and abiding wisdom in the opera.

In Rossini's version, Cinderella has a grandiose stepfather instead of a stepmother. A great teacher and philosopher intervenes on her behalf instead of a fairy godmother. Scott, my younger brother, played the philosopher and wise sage who brought healing. By the end of the opera, he was dressed in dazzling white and made to be the king's wise counsel. He offered Cinderella a transfiguring experience by offering her a new way of life.

I must confess that I still see my younger brother as if we were children. I breathe deeply every time he opens his mouth to sing because I don't want him to fail. I watch the newspapers for reviews of his operatic performances, making sure the reviews are kind and fair. I make sure that he is protected and happy every way I can because I love him deeply. He is the person who makes me proud to be a Lee because of his courage, grit, and determination.

For me, my brother is someone I look up to because to me, he is infinite in his ability to make me laugh, to show me love, and to be the person of ethical hard work that I aspire to be. But it took him reaching his senior year for other colleagues at the school to realize his full potential. By the beginning of the end of his undergraduate career, he has arrived. It's also interesting because Scott was this big football player in high school, but he hurt his shoulder his senior year and needed an activity to participate in. So he started singing, and his velvety bass baritone captured the conservatory that accepted only a handful of students that year. Scott was one of them after only six months of practice.

I tell you this story because we hear a lesson in Mark's Gospel, chapter 9, that is a story of transformation from a first-century rabbi to a Messiah. Jesus has turned his face toward Jerusalem and takes Peter, James, and John with him up a high mountain. And there he is transfigured. He is transformed, like Scott was in *Cinderella*, into a Christological vision with Moses and Elijah.

Now the easy homiletical move in this text is to blame Peter. I know many of you find fault in Peter for wanting to build a dwelling place there, but perhaps we don't give Peter enough credit in Mark's lesson for us today. For in that moment, infinity touched the finite. Or, as the theologian and *Toy Story* character Buzz Lightyear might say, Peter, James, and John were taken to infinity . . . and beyond.

What would you do if heaven touched earth as it does in this account? What might you do if suddenly the prophets of our time showed up with Jesus and had a message for us? I believe the lesson in today's Gospel text is that when heaven bends down to touch earth, you'd best be ready for the beauty of God's infinity. Deeper than that, this is a lesson in touch. Humanity was touched by Christ. I can use my scriptural imagination to see a very ordinary Jesus transformed by the work of the Father bending down and touching Peter on his shoulder and saying, "Peter, don't you see?" For Mark's Gospel is a lesson in not seeing. It's about a bunch of babbling wannabe apostles not getting the message that Jesus is trying to convey until it is long after the fact.

So we too, as wannabe followers of the way of Jesus, fail and forget and forage for answers when the answers to our finite existence are right here in Mark's Gospel. This is made most apparent in today's world because we fail to see the infinity in Jesus, so we settle for finite realities. Evangelicals get in bed with the Trump administration instead of remembering or recollecting that the Spirit of the Lord was upon Jesus because he came to give good news to the poor, not tax cuts to the rich; he came to bring recovery of sight to the blind, not the dismantling of the Affordable Care Act; and he came to let the captive go free, which means closing Guantanamo Bay Prison and reforming our prison industrial complex. In the year of the Lord's favor just a few chapters back, we see that the way we are acting now is an affront to the way Jesus intended. For Jesus came, as did Elijah and Moses, for the sake of the widow and the orphan, the enslaved and the downtrodden, the migrant worker and the Dreamer.

Jesus came as a first-century resident of Palestine to offer us a new way, a different way, a way that says all are welcome in the kingdom of God.

You see, Jesus' transfiguration gives us permission as Christians for a transformation. The issues we face are easily solved in the light of his glory and grace, but it is obvious that the principalities and powers of this world do not see that as a means of solving problems. We are polarized in this nation, and we are a broken empire. But Jesus did not come to save Caesar or the Roman Empire; Jesus entered time as a human being on the outskirts of the empire for the sake of transfiguration.

One of my preaching professors at Duke, Chuck Campbell, said that it is far past time for Christians to call out our leaders, but in so doing we must call out the principalities and powers that make those leaders possible. We must call out the wicked stepfather and stepsisters as in Rossini's *Cinderella*. And I feel that you people here at Memorial Church, under the leadership of your fine clergy, can do just that. You can allow Christ's transfiguration today to lead to a transformation of how you respond to the powerful, the wealthy, and those who wish to dismantle everything we hold dear.

Simply and directly, you must offer to those who claim the finite that you know infinity. You know a God who has made plain that the way of the world is not the way of Christ. You know a God who cares more for the dreamers than those who wish to crush dreams. You know a God who has named racism and xenophobia as sinful. You know a God who sees monuments as idolatrous. So, in that infinite reality, we must name it as part of our finite nature.

With all that said, it can still be difficult. The church is not what she used to be; in fact, many sanctuaries across our country find their pews empty. As Tennyson wrote, "Tho' much is taken, much abides; and tho; / We are not now that strength which in old days / Moved earth and heaven, that which we are, we are—."[58] We may not have the numbers or finances or sheer force we used to have as an institution, but we have infinity and transfiguration on our side. We have Christ our Lord who offers to us a new and different way of seeing the world—a transfigured way of seeing reality. This way, this hope, this reality is what will lead the church and our country to make a way where there is no way.

We must never, ever give up on the possibility of transformation. On this Transfiguration Sunday, may you be resolved to find hope in the reality that we are not the end of the sentence, the paragraph, or the page. We do not write the end of the story, for our God already has. So we must work to bring about that ending in such a way that when all is said and done, we are brought to that table of infinity and of grace.

Some may call me an optimist after hearing these words; some may call me crazy after hearing these words. But let me take you back at least twenty years. I was on a beach with my brother, and my brother got caught under the waves. He told this story at my wedding, and he said that I grabbed him by his shoulders and pulled him back to reality. I asked Scott about that, and he said it was scary for him but he knew I was there and he felt safe knowing that we stuck together. Even in his fear, he knew he had a big brother looking after him and watching out for him. That story for me is an assurance that though the world seems oft so wrong, God is the ruler yet.[59] Scott is now the man I hope that I one day will be, and he's younger than me. He transformed from the young guy under the waves to a strong man who is a star in the North Carolina opera scene.

The hope of the resurrection, the certainty of infinity, is that transfiguration and transformation happen not only in first-century Palestine but in twenty-first-century Statesville, North Carolina, and it can happen in twenty-first-century Cambridge, Massachusetts.

My mom is one of the wisest teachers of Scripture I know, and she joins us here today in this wonderful place. She was the one who first taught my brother and me to love scripture and to hear the song in the heart of God. I remember one day years ago hearing her tell a group of young people that Jesus could have stayed on the mountain like Peter wanted to, but instead he chose to enter back into the world he had come to love to show us the love that made us and makes us one.

---

58. Tennyson, "Ulysses," in *Victorian Poetry and Poetics*, 2nd ed. (Boston: Houghton Mifflin Co., 1959), p. 32, lines 65–67.
59. Maltbie D. Babcock, "This Is My Father's World" (1901).

That is ultimately the message I wish to share with you today. It would have been easy for Scott to have given up after his football injury and not sing. People whispered that he was a wimp for not going back to the field. For us too, it would be easy to silo ourselves off in progressive ivory towers and not engage in the hard work of transformation and transfiguration. But for the sake of the redemption and reconciliation of the world, for the sake of infinity, we must work for a better tomorrow in spite of and in opposition to the powers that wish to see our downfall.

In the end, Jesus did go down the mountain. In the end, I realized that my brother is no longer the kid beneath the waves but a gifted performer and opera singer. I know that in each of these instances and in every instance of grace, God's face is transfigured and made bright in the darkness. For the light shines in the darkness and the darkness could not overcome it.[60] We go down from this mountain to Ash Wednesday, and we go from that day into Lent and into Easter. We have a strong, resilient hope in the transfigured Christ and the future he offers. Or, as Buzz Lightyear would say, "To infinity . . . and beyond."

In the name of God, Father, Son, and Holy Spirit. Amen.

---

60. John 1:5.

EBENEZER BAPTIST CHURCH: THE PULPIT OF DR. KING

MAY 27, 2018

Author's Note: At the invitation of the Rev. Dr. Raphael Warnock, I preached at the Historic Ebenezer Baptist Church—the church that nurtured and was nurtured by the Rev. Dr. Martin Luther King Jr. during the 1960s. This sermon was an attempt to channel the frustration so many of us had at the time. It's also important to note that I was preaching on my first wedding anniversary. I'm grateful Stephanie was gracious enough to attend the service that morning.

Won't you pray with me?

God of our weary years, God of our silent tears, thou who hast brought us thus far along the way, thou who hast by thy might led us into the light, keep us forever in thy path, we pray. O God, may the words of my mouth and the meditation of all our hearts be acceptable in your sight, for you and you alone are our strong rock and our redeemer. Amen.

Will the Atlanta Falcons be the next Shadrach, Meshach, and Abednego? Dear people of God, I came today to talk about a text we have heard before. We've all heard the story of Shadrach, Meshach, and Abednego and the fiery furnace. We've all heard that Nebuchadnezzar was more concerned with the monuments of his time than with the God of Abraham, Isaac, and Jacob. Amid all of this, I want to tell you a story that you may not have heard before and make some comparisons for today.

In 1934, a German soccer team was banned for playing for a year because they would not render the Nazi salute before the start of their game in December 1933. At the start of the fascist regime in Germany, there was the salute, and those who dared to not salute, those who disagreed, those who protested what happened in Germany would later be sent to their deaths at concentration camps across conquered Europe—including the great theologian and thinker Dietrich Bonhoeffer.

Bonhoeffer often spoke of cheap grace, a grace being peddled by Nazi Germany, and a grace being peddled by the Trump Administration today. Bonhoeffer said, "Cheap grace is the grace we bestow on ourselves. Cheap grace is the preaching of forgiveness without requiring repentance, baptism without church discipline, Communion without confession . . . . Cheap grace is grace without discipleship, grace without the cross, grace without Jesus Christ, living and incarnate."[61]

And if you're like me, if you're tired of the status quo we've come to know for the past year, then I invite you to join me in kneeling. Kneeling like Colin Kaepernick, a modern-day prophet in whom we see protest as a form of prophecy.[62] What we need is to wake up to today and see that the National Football League, in an effort to appease the white moderate and the white supremacists, said that kneeling would not take place on their fields without a fine from the league.[63]

Friends, I almost feel like we need to take a collection to pay those fines for the Atlanta Falcons and beyond. For the ones who continue to kneel when the season starts will be like Shadrach, Meshach, and Abednego; they will be thrown into the fiery furnace of Fox News and Breitbart. People will accuse them of being un-American. Well, let me tell you something: if this is America, if America is a place where we can no longer call out white supremacy by kneeling and by protesting, then this is an empire that we must condemn as broken. And we all know what Jesus said about broken empires. We know what happened to Rome.

If the United States of America is willing to negate the First Amendment because white supremacists control the ratings of the NFL, then I think supporters of black life and culture need to reevaluate their relationship

---

61. D. Bonhoeffer, *The Cost of Discipleship*, trans. R. H. Fuller and I. Booth (London: SCM Press, 1959), 36.

62. Steve Wyche, "Colin Kaepernick explains why he sat during national anthem," NFL.com, August 17, 2016 (nfl.com/news/colin-kaepernick-explains-why-he-sat-during-national-anthem-0ap3000000691077).

63. Kevin Seifert and Don Graziano, "New policy requires on-field players, personnel to stand for anthem," ESPN.com, May 23, 2018 (espn.com/nfl/story/_/id/23582533/nfl-owners-approve-new-national-anthem-policy).

with the NFL. I mean, even the fact that owners who are predominately white wealthy men took a vote on those players who are predominately black is a sign that we are headed toward the furnace of fire, and this time God might not save us.

But I didn't come by today to say that all is doom and gloom. I came by today to tell somebody that God is a God who is faithful. God is a God who is deeply concerned with black lives, with immigrant lives, and with indigenous lives. God is so concerned with black lives that God is standing in the fire of police brutality that disproportionately affects black males. God is standing in the fire of the school-to-prison pipeline. God is standing with the slain bodies of people like Trayvon Martin, Michael Brown, and countless others. God has sent prophets and prophetesses like Congressman John Lewis, Jonathan Walton, Raphael Warnock, Bernice King, Kaitlin Curtice, and Bree Newsome. This is God's willingness to stand in the flames with those who suffer and not shrink back.

If anything, we are a people of faith whose lives and livelihoods are threatened by fire—threatened by the fire of white privilege and supremacy. And the very soul of this nation is threatened by a government who has disregarded the other for the sake of themselves. But I know of a Preacher King, the original Dreamer who stood on the steps of the Lincoln Memorial in the 1960s and dreamed of a world where one day the descendant of a slave owner would preach from the same pulpit as the descendant of slaves. So the hope I have to offer today is that we are worshiping together, and no league, no Congress, no president dare try to stop us.

This is our hope: that beyond the supremacy and dangers we face in this movement, we know that God has always and will always be on the side of the oppressed. I call on all of us gathered here under the sound of my voice to speak truth to power about all that is going on in our world. We must give voice to the fact that those who are deemed illegal are being separated from their children in the nation that once said, "Give me your tired, your poor, / Your huddled masses yearning to breathe free."[64]

The beauty of the story is not that God will save us from fire but that God will be with us in the flames. As it has been mentioned, my wife and I are celebrating our one-year wedding anniversary today. Ten months ago today, my wife and I got out of a car and I stood on the stage of the MTV Video Music Awards and said that black lives matter and that the women

---

64. Emma Lazarus, "The New Colossus," poetryfoundation.org/poems/46550/the-new-colossus.

in this country give me hope. That was enough to send my life spiraling into a nightmare of losing my job. But in losing my job, I found my soul. I found new friends and new realities that come with an awakening. What we need in this country right now is a great awakening to the problems of race and class and creed. We need to acknowledge that we have a problem, and God has a solution. It is to kneel when the national anthem is played until the point when all of God's children are found precious in the sight of this government. It is to stand with indigenous people as their lands and livelihoods are being taken away from them, from Alaska to Standing Rock and beyond. It is to say enough is enough to ICE and become a sanctuary for those whom some view as illegal. Let me be clear: black lives, indigenous lives, and immigrant lives are the fabric of this nation. We cannot move forward together until we acknowledge that.

Now I know I'm just a white kid from the Piedmont of North Carolina, but I know deep down that we can work together and find hope in the fact that if I can change, this nation can change. If I can take the Confederate flag down from hanging in my room, then all of us can abandon hopes that the Southern Confederacy will rise again.

When I was little, my babysitter was a black woman some sixty years my senior. Whenever I was falling asleep, she would sing to me that old, old hymn "Sweet Hour of Prayer."[65] You know it: "Sweet hour of prayer, sweet hour of prayer that calls me from a world of care, and bids me at my father's throne, makes all my wants and wishes known." But my babysitter taught me that the sweet hour of prayer she sang about lasted the whole week long. She knew that deep down, the best of all is that God is not done with this world yet. And though she was so ingrained in the Jim Crow era that she wouldn't drink out of the same drinking glasses as our family, she dreamed of a world where we could all be together, where we could all join hands and realize we have far more in common than we do in our differences.

So before I take my seat and have my rest, let me say to you all gathered here today that God is not done with us yet. God knows we are struggling, and I am confident that God will work with us to make things right. But here's the trick: you're going to have to get out and help be the hands and feet of Christ in this world. I heard that down here in Georgia, y'all might make history by electing the first African American female governor. Well, I stopped by today to say we in the South who are of the progressive variety are cheering you on and hoping you in the state of Georgia will

---

65. W. W. Walford, "Sweet Hour of Prayer" (1845).

make history, not just for the state but for what God might do through politicians and preachers, governor's mansions and mother churches like Ebenezer.

We're all in this together. We have not been led this far to be neglected by the God of Jesus Christ, the God who stood in the flames with Shadrach, Meshach, and Abednego. So whether it was through the hushed hope of workers on the Underground Railroad, or the courage of Malcolm X and Martin King, we find that God will raise up leaders for our time. Because ultimately the gospel is the courage and audacity to believe that things can be different. Let me say that again, the gospel is the courage and audacity to believe that things can be different. Church, are you with me? Have you heard the good news that sorrow may last for the night, but joy comes in the morning?[66] Have you heard the good news that Jesus wept in the garden on Thursday and got up out of the tomb on Sunday? Have you heard the good news that if you cannot preach like Peter and you cannot pray like Paul, just tell about the love of Jesus, how he came to save us all?[67] Oh dear people of God, it may seem like the world is falling apart, but maybe in falling apart we will find that God has called us to work to rebuild and reassemble in such a way that white supremacy will no longer be in the vocabulary of this nation, that immigrants will be welcome at the table, and if we don't have enough room we'll build a bigger table.

I know I am not a long-winded preacher, so before I take my seat let me remind you of this: You are precious, Ebenezer Baptist. You are precious, and you are a leader in this community, so it is time for you to lead for the future of Atlanta and the future of Georgia and the future of these United States of America. Because let me tell you a secret. The man who sits at 1600 Pennsylvania Avenue, the modern-day Nebuchadnezzar, is trying to get you to worship the god of the American flag. The question is, will you respond like the Chaldeans did? Or will you respond as Shadrach, Meshach, and Abednego did?

You may say to me that I'm too political for this pulpit, but I know deep down that Jesus was so political it got him killed. Jesus was a zealot for his mission, and it made him an enemy of the state. Deep down, for so long, the black church has been a bulwark of the social gospel of liberation, and it's time we work together until all are welcome and valued here in this land.

---

66. Ps 30:5.

67. Spiritual, "There Is a Balm in Gilead."

Now, as a collateral descendant of Robert E. Lee, I want to say something: I am sorry. I am sorry for the pain the Lee family has caused, and I am sorry that parts of my family tried to keep your ancestors in bondage. But I know that I am going to be a different kind of Robert Lee. I'm going to continue fighting until my last breath for justice, equity, and peace in our land. It is my prayer that you will all join me in the fire and find God there. It is my prayer that you will not yield to Nebuchadnezzar but find God in the flames of the fire. For I know and came to testify that God did not bring us this far to leave us here alone. God is good, and God will bring us out of this mess together on the other side. For there our praise and thanksgiving are found that we will resist, we will not back down, for we are people on a mission and a mission-minded people.

Thanks be to God. Amen.

MARANATHA BAPTIST CHURCH: WITH FORMER PRESIDENT JIMMY CARTER

AUGUST 19, 2018

Won't you pray with me?

God of the one true church, may the words of my mouth and the meditations of all our hearts be pleasing in your sight, for you and you alone are our strong rock and our redeemer. Amen.

My wife Stephanie is a big Bruce Springsteen fan. She loves him for some odd reason. I'm not really that big a fan. But there is one song that I have come to love: "Atlantic City." You may not have heard the lyrics to that song, so let me remind you and jog your memory. Springsteen sings, "Everything dies, baby that's a fact, but maybe everything that dies some day comes back." As I pondered those words this week, I began to ask myself a question: What would I die for? Would I die for your country or what this country represents? Would I die for my friends? Would I die for my spouse? I want you to ponder that today as you prepare to hear God's word proclaimed. Who or what would you die for?

When I was invited to preach today, your pastor Brandon informed me that he wanted me to speak on my first love to study in the field of which I am a part: millennials. Any student of ecclesial matters will tell you that the churches of today are not what they once were in the 1950s.

Diana Butler Bass, a friend of mine and an independent scholar of American Christianity, suggests that for many local congregations, nostalgia is at an all-time high, and many congregations believe the best days are behind them. Broad Street is not immune to that reality, but we are in a position to make a difference. Before you get anxious and decide to tune out, let me explain why I am here today. I believe fully and completely that the church is not done yet. God has not brought us this far to leave us here alone. And though numbers across every church are decreasing, I think we can find some hope in today's gospel lesson.[68]

Today we see that Jesus has come to Caesarea Philippi and he asks his disciples, "Who do people say that the Son of Man is?" The disciples seem to like to avoid answering questions, so like any good person not wanting to pick a fight, they politely answer the question and try to move on. They say, "Some say John the Baptist, but others Elijah, and still others Jeremiah or one of the prophets." Then Jesus points the question directly at them: "Who do you say that I am?" And Simon Peter replies, "You are the Messiah, the Son of the living God." Jesus looks at Peter and says, "And I tell you, you are Peter, and on this rock, I will build my church, and the gates of hell will not prevail against it. I will give you the keys of the kingdom of heaven, and whatever you bind on earth will be bound in heaven, and whatever you loose on earth will be loosed in heaven."

Now before we get too far, I think it's important to point out something we all have missed in reading this text unless you know your biblical archeology well. If you went to Caesarea Philippi and saw this exchange take place, you would see that Jesus himself is standing underneath a massive rock formation. And in that rock formation, which you can still see today, there are massive engravings celebrating the might of the Roman Empire and of its emperor Caesar. There is also a massive hole underneath the rock formation that was known as the gates of Hades. Pagans during this time would throw sacrifices down the hole into what they knew as hell to appease the gods. Jesus was literally pointing to something the disciples would undoubtedly have been scared of and saying this will not prevail against you. What is it that you have to look at and say, "Hell, you will not prevail against me"? For me, it's the future of places like Maranatha Baptist Church and countless other churches I love. I am deeply concerned that the gates of church decline are knocking at our door. But I am not scared because of where Jesus said he would build his church.

---

68. Matt 16:13-20.

Church, do you see where I'm going with this? Jesus had the opportunity to build an empire, and instead he chose to build his church not on the rocks of empire and Caesar but on the likes of a fisherman from Galilee. Jesus had every opportunity to have a church like we had in the 1950s, and he chose to be on the margins with the people who are marginalized, the poor, and the oppressed.

I wrote a book titled *Stained-Glass Millennials*. It focuses on the relationship between the institutional church and millennials. For those of you who may not have heard the word "millennial," these are people born in the 1980s or 1990s. They came of age in the 1990s and early 2000s, witnessed the terror attacks of September 11, 2001, as young people, and have spent most of their lives with the United States and her allies at war. Millennials are for the most part religiously and politically apathetic. Had millennials voted in the same percentage numbers as the rest of the generations, we would have a different president right now, which has led to a political awakening among millennials.[69] But beyond the political sphere, religiously the group of millennials are leaving the church in droves never to return. They are done with religion, and some of them are second-generation "dones"—those people who are classified as being done with organized religion.

All of this makes Jesus' question of "Who do you say that I am?" more pressing. We can no longer sit by and say that Jesus was a nice fellow who did some cool stuff. No, we, like Peter, must proclaim that he is the Son of the living God who changes everything, who takes the nightmare of our existence and makes it the dream of his reality. For Christians today like you and me who want to reach the most religiously disillusioned generation in history, we must confront our own realities. There have been times when we have been judgmental, hypocritical, and played into the stereotypes that make Christians unbearable. But perhaps today when Jesus asks us who he is, we can respond with what millennials and all of us need most: authenticity and vulnerability. We must prepare to face the future with hope, a strong eternal hope that keeps our spirits moving onward and upward toward perfection.

The reality is that the old gray mare, she ain't what she used to be, but God is doing a new and different work in the life of the church. So who

---

69. Polly Mosendz, "What This Election Taught Us about Millennial Voters," Bloomberg.com, November 9, 2016 (bloomberg.com/news/articles/2016-11-09/what-this-election-taught-us-about-millennial-voters).

do you say that Jesus is? Where will you build your church? Will you build it on the reality of stepping out into the great unknown and into God's unfolding future? Or will you stay with the empire humans have built?

You see, what Peter didn't realize in that moment when Jesus calls to him by a different name is what it would cost Simon Peter; it ultimately cost Peter his life. And we too don't realize the implications of church membership when we sign up. We don't realize it will cost us everything. We must engage millennials for our future, even if it makes us uncomfortable. We must engage them not only for the future of the church but also for the future of the salvific nature of God. God in God's goodness loved the whole world so much that when Jesus was raised from the dead, he was raised for baby boomers and millennials alike. Jesus didn't have a test or build a wall by which people could be kept from heaven; he paved the way by which we could bring heaven to earth in the form of Christ's one, holy, apostolic and catholic church. We must be brave enough to answer the question of "Who do you say that I am?" with "You are the Messiah, the Son of the living God. And you came to save millennials just as much as you came to save me."

The experience of salvation tears down the empires we have built and allows us to reach out to the millennial generation. It allows us to reach out to liberals and conservatives, blacks and whites, and everyone in between. In that hope of salvation, we see that authenticity and vulnerability are at the heart of God and should be at the heart of the church as well.

At Duke, there is a theologian named Stanley Hauerwas who was named by *Time* magazine as the greatest theologian of our time. Dr. Hauerwas has had an incredible influence on me, and he even endorsed my book on millennials. But Dr. Hauerwas also challenged us at Duke and has this one line that has been getting to me lately. He says, "Jesus didn't tell you you'd get out of life alive. He just gave you something worth dying for."

Friends, these old walls have their stories. But the beauty of God is that our hope lies not in the past but in what lies ahead. Yes, the future of the church is bleak, but you are Maranatha Baptist Church. You are a church who must engage millennials for the sake of the salvation of the world, and the gates of hell will not prevail against you because you are the church of God made manifest here in Plains, Georgia. Hell will not prevail against you because they will know you are Christians by your love. Not by your condemnation and dismay, but by hope and a brighter tomorrow.

Dear people of God, this place and the Lord of this place are worth dying for. This place and its Lord are worth dying to the old way of doing things for the sake of God's unfolding future. This place and its Lord are worth giving our lives to for the sake of millennials who just need a good word from the people of God. They don't need platitudes or half-truths; they need people like you who are willing to die to the old way to give birth to the new. To make room for the resurrection of Jesus Christ and of his church. Or, as Bruce Springsteen so aptly put it, "Everything dies, baby that's a fact, but maybe everything that dies some day comes back." Who do you say that Jesus is? Take heart: he, like Bruce Springsteen, has come back. Amen, and amen.

SUMMING UP MY ONE SERMON

> *I didn't go to religion to make me happy. I always knew a bottle of Port would do that. If you want a religion to make you feel really comfortable, I certainly don't recommend Christianity.*
> —C. S. Lewis (from God in the Dock)

I saved these columns for last—they cover my career, and no matter their age they have a cherished vintage that show God never gave up on me. God will never give up on me. And it's in that realization that I continue the work and never, ever give up.

FAITH IN APPALACHIA: A LESSON IN STORYTELLING

OCTOBER 22, 2013

The cultural identity of the place I call home is about as complicated as the roads it takes to get here. I grew up in the shadow of the Appalachian Mountains, I attend a university that bears the name of this region, and I serve a church that has its fabric ingrained within the mountains we know as home. If you ask someone what it means to be from the region known as Appalachia, you will receive as many different answers as the trees in the Shenandoah Valley. You could get the "official" answer based on a map (though there are a few maps that like to be called official). You could get your answer based on your dialect, your sense of place, or your love for this land. I have come to know a different definition: when you tell the stories that make these mountains move their ear to listen, you know what it means to be from Appalachia.

The stories I hear every Sunday when the community I serve gathers for worship are a lesson in faith. I've heard stories of how one church member's great-grandfather was baptized in a river not far from here in 1888. I've heard the heart-wrenching stories of families losing livelihoods due to the expansion of civilization throughout these hills. I've seen the joy of the tenacious ability to have a mountain festival honoring everything from apples to woolly worms.

Appalachia inspires stories, and stories inspire faith. I often wonder if the great faiths of the world could take a lesson from the people in this region. What would it look like if faith traditions could get back to the root of the stories they've come to know? Much of the conversation we have today is commentary on the story; we talk theology as if it is the spring of everything we hold dear. The reality is that all of us involved with a faith tradition are people intertwined with a story. We are human beings built with an existence that has been around long before we ever came along.

If you've ever been to my neck of the woods in Appalachia, you will have experienced the majestic beauty of the New River. I have the privilege of seeing it every day on my way to work, and though there is nothing new about this river (it's the third oldest in the world), I've often marveled at the sensation of watching the river go its course throughout the gorge it carved out even before the Nile River or Amazon River came along. One of my church members compares life to the New River—the winding twists and turns, the overwhelming terror and grace that life will continue to run through that gorge long after we're gone.

Our lives are haunted and charted by our stories. If serving a church in Appalachia has taught me one thing, it is the authentic hope of telling our stories in such a way that they will be passed on to posterity. The stories, both big and small, are a reminder that the chain of time is not disconnected but is intricately woven into our beings. We are built by the stories we have come to live with. Ask anyone in Appalachia about the stories of their childhood, the blizzard of 1950, the mountaintop removal, or the chestnut trees now committed only to memory, and you will hear a story about their very soul. For they have all come to know lessons in grace, hope, love, forgiveness, charity, and justice through living the experiences that taught them who they are and ultimately whose they are.

I want to be careful not to iconize this area as a land of milk and honey where the stories are always as beautiful as the view from the front porch. Let me be clear: some of these stories are painful tales of the reality of living in an impoverished area of our country. The county I work in has the highest suicide rate in the entire state; there have been months without sun or warm weather. This is still very much the frontier in some regards, but ultimately that is what faith is anyway.

Faith is the frontier land of our existence in that faith calls us to go, to journey, to explore, to remind ourselves of what we consider important and valuable. Faith is the land just beyond the ridge that yearns for us to explore it. It was William Blake who said, "Great things happen when men and mountains meet."[70] In this confluence of nature, culture, and history

---

70. From Gnomic Verses in *Verse and Prose by William Blake*, c. 1850, rossettiarchive.org/docs/3-1862.blms.rad.html.

meeting the human element, we see the beauty of faith. Won't you join me on this journey to the heart of our story and the frontier of our intermingling with the Divine? Or, as John Muir said, "The mountains are calling, and I must go."[71]

---

71. Muir to his sister, Sarah Muir Galloway, September 3, 1873. In *To Yosemite and Beyond: Writings from the Years 1863–1875* (Salt Lake City: University of Utah Press, 1999), 152.

THE ADVENT OF THE STARS

DECEMBER 2011

There is something about being a college student in which the spontaneity of life overtakes you. One night, in the early hours of the morning, a small group of friends here at Appalachian decided that we wanted an adventure. We gathered blankets and jackets and set out on the Blue Ridge Parkway. We ended up at the Julian Price Memorial Park along the banks of Price Lake. We sat along the banks of the lake and marveled at the stars that peeked out from the canopy of clouds.

I started a conversation with a friend whom I have come to love, and we talked about the meaning of our existence. We looked across the lake and saw the beauty of the stars light years away. I couldn't help but feel God at work in our lives, mending, creating, restoring while we were watching the stars. I was reminded of words frequently attributed to Martin Luther: "God writes the Gospel not in the Bible alone, but also on trees, and in the flowers and clouds and stars."

God was at work in the early hours of a Monday when we all had tests and assignments to do later that morning. You could feel the tangible evidence of God's grace at work in the conversations going on. Our pasts, our histories, were revealed in a different light, and our futures looked a little brighter. Maybe it was Orion's Belt shining in the darkness, but I tend to cling to the hope that it was God in our midst.

Eventually we realized we needed to head back to the university and get some sleep. As we drove back to Boone, we could see the twinkling of the city coming into view. I thought of that wonderful town, of how God came long ago to save the likes of us. I thought of Advent, which is quickly approaching, in which with great expectancy we await the coming Christ.

After I dropped my friends off and was heading back to my dorm, I was listening to the radio. Christmas music was on, and one of my favorite carols was playing. The wonderful line, "Yet in thy dark streets shineth the everlasting Light, the hopes and fears of all the years are met in thee tonight."

Within the streets of towns and cities, God is at work. The hopes of our lives and the fears of our existence are brought into a different light in the presence of the incarnate Savior. God is bringing about God's reign through ordinary experiences like stargazing.

As we approach the Advent season, as we approach the beauty of everything we hold dear, may we always remember the experiences that make this time special. Whether that be a late-night adventure with friends, a feast on our tables, or the wonders of this time, may we always find God amid our ordinary existence.

LET'S FOCUS ON THE REAL CONVERSATION

SEPTEMBER 11, 2017

Note from newspaper editor: The Rev. Rob Lee, a Statesville native, recently resigned his pastorship due to backlash caused by his appearance on MTV's Video Music Awards. This column was written by Lee and his wife, Stephanie, in response.

We first met over newsprint. We first met in the Appalachian newspaper office on the campus of our alma mater. You could say we're familiar with headlines. The headlines we've been reading lately are frustrating because dialogues that openly address the divisions in our country are being put on the back burner to talk about a disagreement.

People holding Nazi flags marched in Charlottesville, called to action by the removal of a statue of Rob's ancestor. That conversation has seemed to slip into obscurity. Blame the media all you want, but when readership spikes for the online story that says "Pastor loses job" and falls on "Pastor calls for uncomfortable change," then the message is clear: everyone wants to read about someone else's discomfort and not their own. *This* is what has happened. It is a plague on our nation. And it detracts from meaningful change and discussion.

Privilege is knowing that you have lost your job and that you will be okay. The future may not be what you thought it would be: the credit card debt won't be paid off this month, the spending money will go away, and choices will have to be made. But surviving a devastating blow is privilege.

The question we face now as a community is not whether Rob resigned or the circumstances surrounding it, but instead how the church will continue to be a bulwark of strength for people who need the church the most.

Let's shift the headline to something different. Let's shift it to where we could come together on the issues that matter or begin conversations surrounding racist statutes and statues that hinder growth, as the Rev. William Barber says. Let's talk about DACA and the Dreamers. Let's listen without judging, and realize that beloved community is possible. We don't have to agree on everything, but we can no longer turn a blind eye to injustice.

Perhaps by focusing on these conversations, the conversations that matter, we will then come to know the awesome grace of God. Perhaps then we shall recognize the liberating force of the God who brought the Israelites to freedom through the sea. Perhaps then we shall see that this message isn't about a person who resigned but about not being afraid to have the tough conversations surrounding racism. May God richly bless all of us in this endeavor.

OUR LIVES ARE DEFINED BY LOVE

AUGUST 8, 2014

The prolific author Wendell Berry turned eighty this week. In one of his essays he writes,

> I take literally the statement in the Gospel of John that God loves the world. I believe that the world was created and approved by love; that it subsists, coheres, and endures by love, and that, insofar as it is redeemable, it can be redeemed only by love. I believe that divine love, incarnate and indwelling in the world, summons the world towards wholeness which is ultimately reconciliation and atonement with God.[72]

It is the reality of our time that we could all use a little more love. Whatever conflict our world faces today is cured and absorbed by love. Whether it is the conflict over Palestinian territory, the Ebola crisis, or gridlock here at home, we have the opportunity to be transfixed by the changing power of a God who embraces us with God's love.

To take literally the love God has for us, we must begin to look toward our unity rather than our divisions. We must begin to embrace each other rather than refraining from embracing. To bask in the love of God, we must find ourselves truly realized in the hope of the resurrection and the light of eternity. We must love the God who loves us.

Dear friends, it is not just enough to bask in the light of love; we have to share it as well. We are called to love because, as Berry says, that is what will redeem the world. This week, I challenge you to fight injustice

---

72. *Another Turn of the Crank* (Berkeley: Counterpoint, 2011), 89.

and oppression with love, and fight the terror of this world with love and hope—the durable forces that unite us all.

God is love; where love is, there God is also. The heart of life is the love of God, and God is good.

www.ingramcontent.com/pod-product-compliance
Lightning Source LLC
Chambersburg PA
CBHW051119160426
43195CB00014B/2261